Practical Wisdom 1

In Real Life and Management

Kochouseph Chittilappilly

Viva Books
New Delhi | Mumbai | Chennai | Kolkata | Bengaluru | Hyderabad | Kochi | Guwahati

Publisher's note

Every possible eff ort has been made to ensure that the infomation contained in this book is accurate at the time of going to press, and the publisher and author cannot accept responsibility for any errors or omissions, however caused. No responsibility for loss or damage occasioned to any person acting, or refraining from action, as a result of the material in this publication can be accepted by the editor, the publisher or the author.

Every effort has been made to trace the owners of copyright material used in this book. The author and the publisher will be grateful for any omission brought to their notice for acknowledgement in the future editions of the book.

First Published 2013
Reprinted 2014, 2016

Viva Books Private Limited

- 4737/23, Ansari Road, Daryaganj, New Delhi 110 002
  Tel. 42242200, 23258325, 23283121, Email: vivadelhi@vivagroupindia.net
- 76, Service Industries, Shirvane, Sector 1, Nerul, Navi Mumbai 400 706
  Tel. 27721273, 27721274, Email: vivamumbai@vivagroupindia.net
- Megh Tower, Old No. 307, New No. 165, Poonamallee High Road, Maduravoyal, Chennai 600 095
  Tel. (044) 23780991, 23780992, Email: vivachennai@vivagroupindia.net
- B-103, Jindal Towers, 21/1A/3 Darga Road, Kolkata 700 017
  Tel. 22816713, Email: vivakolkata@vivagroupindia.net
- 7, GF, Sovereign Park Aptts., 56-58, K. R. Road, Basavanagudi, Bengaluru 560 004
  Tel. 26607409, Email: vivabangalore@vivagroupindia.net
- 101-102, Moghal Marc Apartments, 3-4-637 to 641, Narayanguda, Hyderabad 500 029
  Tel. 27564481, Email: vivahyderabad@vivagroupindia.net
- First Floor, Beevi Towers, SRM Road, Kaloor, Kochi 682 018
  Tel. 0484-2403055, 2403056, Email: vivakochi@vivagroupindia.net
- 232, GNB Road, Beside UCO Bank, Silpukhuri, Guwahati 781 003
  Tel. 0361-2666386, Email: vivaguwahati@vivagroupindia.net

www.vivagroupindia.com

ISBN: 978-81-309-2398-7

Edited by:
Prof. T.P. Antony

Illustrated by
Prakash Shetty

Published by Vinod Vasishtha for Viva Books Private Limited, 4737/23 Ansari Road, Daryaganj, New Delhi 110 002.

Printed and bound by Raj Press, R-3, Inderpuri, New Delhi 110 012.

M0200/M0457/M0454/M0350

Dedication

I dedicate this book to my parents C.O. Thomas and Mariamma Thomas who taught me, right from childhood, the importance of straightforwardness, hard work and positive thinking. It was they who showed me, that peace of mind is more important than money. I learned from their lives, that acceptance in society and a concern for people are essential for success in life.

The profits from the sale of this book will be utilised only for charitable purposes.

Table of Contents

	Foreword	*vii*
	Preface	*ix*
	The origin of the book	*xi*
1.	Recipe for success	1
2.	Successful personality	3
3.	Positive thinking	5
4.	Self-confidence	7
5.	Delegation	10
6.	Empowerment	12
7.	Thoughts and character	14
8.	Happiness	16
9.	Emotional intelligence	18
10.	Emotional stability	20
11.	Right attitude	22
12.	True happiness	24
13.	Real success	26
14.	Ignite your inner power	28
15.	Be fair and firm	30
16.	Truth begets courage	32
17.	Nobody can make you inferior without your consent	34
18.	Forgive and forget	36
19.	Analyse the effectiveness of each work	38
20.	Be inquisitive	40
21.	Your personality is reflected in your deeds	42
22.	Rule over challenge and controversy	44
23.	Trust, to get the best	46
24.	Live in the present	48
25.	Realise your strength	50

26.	Perseverance can make wonders happen	52
27.	Pygmalion effect	54
28.	Integrated success formula	56
29.	People manager	58
30.	Education – the parrot's way!	60
31.	Evils of unbridled freedom	63
32.	Shame shame!	65
33.	Survival of the fittest	67
34.	Necessity is the mother of invention	69
35.	A short pen is better than a long memory	71
36.	Lead a happy family life	73
37.	Discipline and etiquette	75
38.	Entrepreneurial tranquillity	77
39.	Standing out in a world of look-alikes	79
40.	Liberalisation	81
41.	The bane of productivity	83
42.	Money order economy	85
43.	Hardcore self motivation	87
44.	Brand name	89
45.	Branding – a careful approach	91
46.	Brand building	94
47.	Poor self-esteem	97
48.	A satisfied customer is the best advertising medium	100
49.	Hostage at home	102
50.	Do your duties first	105
51.	There is strength in numbers	107
52.	Luck and ill-luck	110
	About the Author	112

Foreword

One of the things we should learn from the west is to read and write. Indians are weak in documentation. They have so much to share and so much to give to others; if only they sit to write, there can be volumes written on many things that can change life or give new perspectives. That is one of the reasons why we don't have Indian psychology well developed and quoted in the west. But we have great minds.

In this book the author Kochouseph Chittilapilly has done a great service to people by documenting simple truths drawn from his own personal experiences and the experience of his company – V-Guard. It is a pleasure to read this book. Simple truths told from experience and wrapped into wisdom drawn from the familiar. Can you re-tell the story of the Hare and the Tortoise and draw lessons on globalization that competent people win if they are only a little more careful in putting their competencies to use, than rotting them?

What makes you successful? What are the symptoms of an optimist? How do you stop minority from destroying the peace of the majority? What can satisfied customers do to you? These are the kinds of questions answered in this book through incidents and short stories. This book also deals with issues like: Delegation, Empowerment, Talent Identification, Forgiveness, Happiness, Inquisitiveness, Emotional stability, Trust, etc.

Carrying a scribbling pad and a pen should become a part of life. So is the discipline of recording important things. The book is well written with simple illustrations and live experiences. I am sure the readers will enjoy reading the simple truths told in an interesting way, like stories. I congratulate Kochouseph Chittilapilly, Managing Director of V-Guard Industries for writing this book for use by everyone. It makes an easy and useful reading. I hope some of the readers will also take inspiration from Kochouseph Chittilapilly and start documenting their experiences.

Dr. T. V. Rao — Former Chairman, TVRLS, Ahmedabad
(Formerly Professor – HR, IIM [Ahmedabad])

Preface

This book has evolved from a collection of my thoughts, observations and evaluations, which I have jotted down over the last several years. These are based on lessons I have drawn from my own experiences, and an analysis of people who have achieved success in various fields. I never dreamt that I would one day write a book on management thoughts! Frankly speaking, I have no formal training in management, and I am no expert on management theories. I had to write, in order to communicate my thoughts to our managers and staff, who are geographically dispersed in various places.

I never expected that my little efforts would have such an outcome. In all humility, I now recall what the Bhagavad Gita says about duty, कर्मण्येवाधिकारस्ते मा फलेषु कदाचन. Do your duty, and never expect to receive the fruits of your labour, which will come in its own way. This time, I got my reward in the form of a book.

Our managers and staff have put in a lot of effort at the various stages during the compilation of my random thoughts into this book. I studied in a Malayalam medium school, and those who know me well, would know that English grammar and spelling have never been my forte. I still remember my days at school where I was punished by my English teachers for not doing well enough in English. Sad to say, all their efforts were in vain! The material for this book has been edited, corrected and made presentable, by many who have contributed to the process of putting it together.

Many people believe that the 'V' in our brand name stands for 'We'. At the functional level, it is the concept of 'We', which is the driving force behind 'V-Guard'. Teamwork is the secret of our success. Through this book, 'We' have once again proved our strength. A list of the names of all those who helped to put together this book, would run into several pages. I express my heartfelt thanks to all of them for their sincere efforts. A special word of thanks to all those who consented to write their opinions about the book, and also wrote the Foreword. Once again, I thank everyone involved, especially those who encouraged and motivated me to keep writing my thoughts, and many others who were in some way, involved in publishing this book.

Kochouseph Chittilappilly

The origin of the book

When I look back over the years, I feel that it would be right to compare my little efforts with the good old adage in Malayalam 'പല തുള്ളി പെരുവെള്ളം' which means, 'Many drops of water make a mighty ocean.' In 1996, during the discussions that followed at the end of a training programme that I was conducting for our managers and officers, one of our managers in the Q.A. department gave me a new idea. "Sir, why not write about your management thoughts and practical experiences in 'V & We', our in-house magazine". Inspired by those words I started writing articles in 'V & We' on a monthly basis, and this has become a regular feature in the magazine.

After a few months I was worried that my stock of ideas was about to be exhausted. But by then, the articles had been well accepted by the readers, and the words of appreciation from many different people, motivated me to keep writing regularly. The editorial board of 'V & We' had requested me to submit my material by the 20th of every month; something which has put a little extra pressure on me to ensure that I come out with a new article every month.

Much water has flowed under the bridge since then. In fact in 2002, six years after I started my column in V&We, another manager from Veega Land (Now re-named Wonderla, Kochi) said to me one day, "Sir, you have written more than 50 articles so far, and there is now enough material to be compiled into a book". Although I found the idea appealing, I had some apprehensions about whether there would be any readers for the book. One day, during a casual conversation with the noted Malayalam writer, Mr. K. L. Mohanavarma, I discussed this suggestion to have the articles compiled into a book. He took great interest in the proposal, collected the file which contained all my articles, and carefully read through all of them. Having done that, he said to me, "This will definitely prove to be useful material for entrepreneurs, managers and management students, who will find it a good source of some simple and practical management tips". Even though it has taken seven long years, I now find myself privileged to be elevated to a special category, as the author of a book!

1

Recipe for success

All of us agree that hard work is essential to become a successful person. We come across a good number of hardworking people around us. But many of them are not successful in life. Why do they fail to achieve success? To be successful, hard work should blend harmoniously with new ideas, to form a potent combination. Unless we generate new ideas, we cannot survive in this fast-changing, competitive world. This process will enable us not only to reduce our workload, but also provide us with the essential mental happiness.

Ideas hover around us unknown or unnoticed. An alert mind can catch them and tap them to the best advantage.

Nothing under the sun is new. Ideas hover around us unknown or unnoticed. An alert mind can catch them and tap them to the best

The human mind is like a parachute. It will not work unless it is open.

advantage. The human mind is like a parachute. It will not work unless it is open. We must feel the pressure to generate new ideas.

I would like to cite a small example. Whenever our relatives came to Kochi, they visited us before visiting other relatives. This happened frequently since our house is located on a prominent road. Every time, it was my wife's duty to conduct them to the houses of other relatives because the guests were not familiar with the roads in Kochi. In this way, a lot of her time available for renewing social contact was wasted in giving them directions. To solve this recurring problem, she prepared a route map showing the location of relatives' houses and ensured that enough number of copies were made available. It was in itself a simple act, but it was a true innovation. She just opened her mind and it opened up the way to find a solution to her problem.

Now she finds ample time to socialise with our relatives in a relaxed manner. Looking back, she wishes that the idea should have dawned upon her much earlier!

I have cited this small instance to convey the idea that new ideas will help to reduce one's workload considerably. To generate new ideas, four conditions must be fulfilled.

1. One must feel the pressure of the workload to the extent of a problem.
2. There must be strong belief that there will be a solution to any problem, i.e. a more simple alternative.
3. An open mind to search for alternative solutions to any problem.
4. Selection of the best alternative and proper implementation of the same.

Follow the rules; success will be yours!

2

Successful personality

In an interview, the reporter of a leading newspaper asked me an important question, "Can you define a successful personality?" This was an unexpected question and my reply was not to my complete satisfaction. After that, for a number of days, I tried to find out a clear definition for a 'successful personality' whether he is a businessman, industrialist, manager, supervisor or somebody else. As a result of careful observation of several leaders and many successful personalities, I arrived at four major criteria to assess a successful personality. The assessment is based on answers to the following questions.

1. Does he have proper mental peace and happiness?
2. Is he physically fit, considering his age?
3. Is he well accepted in society?
4. Is he financially stable?

If the answers to all the four questions are 'yes', then he is definitely a successful person. If the answer is negative to even one of these questions, he is not a successful person. Many people wrongly think that money is the main criterion to judge whether a person is successful or not. In my opinion, money has only a one fourth role in a successful man's life. I have come across a beautiful sentence in a book, 'The richest man in the world is he who is happy with the least comfort.' Some people you know may be immensely rich. But they may not have mental peace and happiness. The costliest bed in the world cannot offer them good sleep. Of what use is it to you, if you capture the entire world but are unable to sleep in peace?

Money has only a one fourth role in a successful man's life.

Another category of people run after money without caring for their health. They may be having a very good bank balance, which will be useful for the next generation. But in the process of making money, these poor people acquire many illnesses like blood pressure, peptic ulcer, cervical spondylosis, etc. Can we say they are successful? Definitely not. Yet another category of people earn money through ways like smuggling, black marketing or corruption. They may score three of the four points in the checklist. But what about their acceptance in the society?

When I examine myself, I find that I have very good mental peace and happiness. I also get very good sleep at night. Please do not think I am overrating myself if I say that I am physically fitter than many people of my age. Am I well accepted in society? You decide.

3

Positive thinking

> Work hard, making use of available facilities and win over difficult situations. This is the right path to success.

Success follows an optimist. An optimist will find an opportunity in every difficulty and a pessimist will see a difficulty in every opportunity. Opportunities are in plenty, and are flying around us from all directions. We have to open our eyes wide to see them and grab them. Be assured that in every difficulty there is a hidden advantage. Let me share with you my own experience. The labour situation in Kerala was not very encouraging during the period between 1984 and 1988. We were also encountering a number of labour problems. There was a general feeling in Kerala that the labour situation and trade union militancy were retarding industrial growth in the state. Many industrialists were disgusted with the situation and they decided to stop their activities in Kerala.

My approach to the problem was different. I saw light in the darkness created by such problems. To tackle the situation we started subcontracting our work to some social organisations. Gradually, our efforts were met with success. My firm conviction is that one has to face the difficulties and find a solution to the problem by adopting alternative means. How can we think of alternative means if we cannot think positively? To cite yet another instance, we had bitter experiences from various government agencies way back in 1986. But then, to counter this, we became cautious and systematic in maintaining our records, which proved to be a blessing in disguise. Today, all our records are up-to-date.

Friends, we have to find comfort in the available facilities and then try to improve upon them. If one simply dreams of a situation where no problems exist, I would say he is foolish. We live in a competitive world, full of challenges. Fight them all using a weapon called OPTIMISM. This is the right attitude to tide over a problem.

The difference between optimism and pessimism can be illustrated by a simple example. There are two persons who are thirsty and we offer them each half a glass of cool water. A pessimist or a man with negative thinking will say, "How unfortunate I am! I have got only half a glass of water." On the other hand, an optimist or a positive thinker will say, "How fortunate I am! I have got at least half a glass

of water." The situation and the facility available are the same to both of them. But, look at the way they see things. Discontent with the available facility or cursing one's own fate and waiting for a lucky break is not the correct approach to life. Work hard, making use of the available facilities and win over difficult situations. This is the right path to success.

Analyse any success story and you will see that luck plays only a very minor role. The basic ingredient of success is positive thinking.

4

Self-confidence

During a presentation, one of the delegates asked me, "You have singled out the importance of individuals and their self-confidence as the key factors of success. But what about team work and delegation of power?"

Team work and delegation of power are certainly important factors that contribute to one's success.

Yes, team work and delegation of power too are certainly important factors that contribute to one's success. But, to be able to delegate assignments to others, you must have faith in others. In order to have faith in others, first of all, you must have faith in yourself. Only mentally balanced persons can trust others.

If you are afraid of delegating powers to others, it clearly indicates that you lack self-confidence. Moreover, you will always be obsessed by the feeling that all others will cheat you. If someone says that he has no faith in others, it simply means that he is basically incompetent.

The plight of Galileo, who was imprisoned for declaring that the Earth revolves around the Sun.

We can easily identify assertive people from the tone of their voice, and gestures. Their voice levels will be generally higher than those with less self-confidence. Even from a telephone conversation we can easily make out whether the person at the other end is smart or just mediocre. A person's facial expressions also clearly indicate whether he or she is shy and inhibited, or an extrovert.

During group discussions, diffident people find it difficult even to express their ideas. These people have many inhibitions. They may have new ideas. But they think that their ideas may be foolish and others will laugh at them. Please remember that many such 'foolish' ideas have eventually become a reality and changed the course of history.

Take the case of Galileo. He was the first person who proclaimed: "The Earth revolves around the Sun." Until then, the whole world believed that the Sun revolved around the Earth. Everyone thought that Galileo had made a foolish statement. He was accused of misguiding people and challenging religious faith, and was imprisoned by the Catholic Church. In those days the Catholic Church was very powerful in Italy and it was virtually ruling the country. The Church believed that God created the earth first and then created the Sun to provide light and heat!

In Galileo I find a man full of self-confidence, a man who trusted himself. Otherwise, he would not have had the courage to utter such a 'foolish' and rebellious statement and stick to his words defying the punishment. Hundreds of years have passed since then. Now we respect him as a great discoverer, who created a major turning point in the study of astronomy.

What I am trying to impress upon you is the role of self-confidence in every success story. To help you build self-confidence I have a capsule for you. Every morning and evening, in a serene and peaceful atmosphere, close your eyes and proclaim loudly the following statements.

1. I trust myself more than anybody else.
2. I am as competent as any other person.
3. I will work hard to achieve my goals.
4. I am more confident today than I was yesterday.

Some people may think that this is foolish advice. But I am sure that its regular practice will bring about a change in your attitude to life and work, and that this will mark a turning point in your life.

5

Delegation

> We must have the patience to motivate our subordinates to bring out their real talent.

A successful manager is one who knows the art of delegation. However, before delegating powers, superiors must have complete trust in the capabilities of their subordinates. I strongly believe that all human beings have many latent talents. No one knows for certain how much dynamism exists in each person. Usually, one develops heroic courage, which has gone unnoticed earlier, during certain crisis situations.

Every man is born with enormous potential. But all this lies hidden deep within him. The importance of correct upbringing during childhood, cannot be over-emphasised. Due to lack of proper guidance or the absence of right opportunities, many of our talents remain dormant or latent within us.

This reminds me of the story of a lion cub that lost his way and was separated from his mother. The lion cub finally landed up in a herd of sheep. Since the cub was very small and was crying for help, the herd accepted him. After a few days, the lion cub started eating grass and imitating the sheep's cry by making bleating sounds instead of roaring like a lion. Nobody had taught him how to roar, showing his canines. His posture, gait, etc. were exactly like those of a sheep. Day and night, he ate and slept with the herd. He soon became very timid and passive like a sheep.

Meanwhile, the mother lioness was searching for her cub. One day she identified her cub among the sheep, retrieved him and took him

back to her den. Gradually, he developed all the vitality and vigour of a real lion cub. Within a few days he became very aggressive and smart.

This story tells us how circumstances influence all living beings. This is true in the case of human beings also. This truth is easily noticed in typical college hostels. Among those who enrol for the Pre-Degree, those who come from the villages can be easily made out. They will be very shy and timid in the initial days. But those who come from towns, or those who have stayed in boarding schools previously, show smartness and aggressiveness from the very first day. By the end of the academic year, we find that some of the so-called 'shy' students from the villages have become as smart as those from towns and show their real talent.

If we give opportunities to our subordinates we can see the astonishing transformation taking place in their outlook and approach. We must have the patience to motivate them so as to bring out their real talent.

6
Empowerment

If we wish to entrust a particular task to our subordinates, we must first of all repose confidence in them, and have faith in their ability to complete the task in a better manner. Before that can take place, the details of the task should be properly discussed with them and their suggestions should be taken into account. We need to explain to them the objective of that particular task, and the reason for adopting a particular method to do it. It is always better to get the opinions of one's subordinates, on whether there is an alternative method, better than the one suggested.

It is always better to get the opinions of one's subordinates, on whether there is an alternative method, better than the one suggested.

Some managers, who never allow their subordinates to express their views, complain later, "I am not getting any co-operation

Delegation of work does not mean simply dumping the workload on the shoulders of one's subordinate.!!?

from my subordinates." Do you think he will get full support from others? Certainly not. A person doing his job with a hundred percent involvement makes a lot of difference. For anyone to involve himself wholeheartedly in a task, his ideas should be taken into account. Any intelligent human being will be somewhat reluctant to implement an idea which was fully conceived by another person. So, merely dictating the procedures will not yield any useful results.

Some people who wield authority, convey an attitude that says, "You just do this. Don't argue with me; I am more experienced in this field." If this is our attitude, we will never get the wholehearted co-operation of our subordinates. In such cases, we are not allowing them to think for themselves and contribute their ideas. If some of their suggestions are accepted, they will work hard to prove themselves correct.

Delegation of work does not mean just dumping the workload on the shoulders of one's subordinates. On the other hand, collective discussions will do wonders for the growth of the organisation. Remember that sometimes even the most inexperienced, junior member, may come up with wonderful and simple ideas. Everyone should be made to feel that his own views have been taken note of.

In many books on management we come across a common term called 'Empowerment'. It means that employees are empowered to take decisions at their level and do not have to go to their boss or supervisor frequently for approval. Since wise decisions are taken by knowledgeable employees at all levels, top executives find ample time to plan future steps and think creatively. I strongly believe that this is the secret behind the growth of the V-Guard group.

7

Thoughts and character

> A man can rise, conquer and achieve things only by lifting up his thoughts.

I was under a sort of house arrest for a few days because of chicken pox. It was a blessing in disguise because I found time to read a beautiful and meaningful book on 'Thoughts and Character'. The book clearly explains that a man is literally what he thinks; his character being the complete sum of all his thoughts. Actions blossom from thoughts. Joy and suffering are the fruits. The human mind is like a garden which can be intelligently developed or allowed to run wild. If no useful seeds are planted, a lot of useless weeds will grow.

You can notice that a few among us are in the habit of criticising and complaining about everything. They always find fault with their family members, colleagues, neighbours and so on. They complain even about their own health, their figure, fate, etc. and curse themselves. Normally, the public will avoid such people. When they get alienated from society, they will start blaming it, and will find all sorts of excuses to justify their line of thinking. An open-minded look at things will lead us to the conclusion that everything depends upon our own attitude. Living in similar set of circumstances with the same facilities, some are happy while others are unhappy. It is obvious that attitudes make all the difference.

All of us want our circumstances to improve. But we are unwilling to improve ourselves. In fact, our attitude always is: "Let society improve first. After that I will improve myself." If everyone thinks in this way, society will never change. We generally bewail that politicians

We are prisoners of our own thoughts. The door is locked from the inside, by us.

are good for nothing, that corruption is at its peak level, and that bureaucracy and red-tapism are the curse of the country. At the same time, we do not hesitate to offer bribes, to follow unfair methods to get our children admitted to a college, to secure recommendations to get a job, to violate traffic rules or to adopt measures we openly disapprove of. A man cannot directly choose his circumstances but he can choose his thoughts and so indirectly, yet surely, shape his circumstances.

If someone worries that he is physically weak, his health will deteriorate further. If a student has a strong notion that he is not at all intelligent, how can he perform well in the examinations? Clearly, we are the prisoners of our own thoughts. The door is locked from inside by us. Nobody from outside can help us in such situations. A man can rise, conquer and achieve things only by lifting up his thoughts. He will only remain weak and miserable if he refuses to do so. Just as a physically weak person can make himself strong by careful and patient physical training, a mentally weak person can tone up his mind with the right thought processes. For, it was high thinking and plain living that have made our ancient Rishis invulnerable.

8

Happiness

Laugh and the world laughs with you, weep and you weep alone.

Self-discipline and lasting happiness are inter-related. For example, if a rich person thinks that no one is going to question him if he consumes three or four pegs of whisky daily, or eats a large quantity of rich food, he may find temporary happiness. But sooner or later he will realise that his unhealthy habits are driving him fast to "Yamapuri".

Unhealthy food habits may cause serious health problems.

I have a habit of observing and analyzing successful and happy people. In the process, I have noticed that they have some common traits. Here are some of my observations:

1. *Happy people are successful in what they do.* All of them like their jobs. They find great pleasure in whatever they do. They are always

willing to try out new avenues. Because of their positive attitude, they will be able to overcome any crisis situation.

2. *Happy people enjoy better health.* Generally, their physical health is very sound. Some of them may be suffering from certain chronic diseases or disabilities. But they have no time to think about their physical condition. They tend to lead happy lives. Gradually, the severity of their illness reduces.
3. *Happy people are liked by others.* They always have a smiling face and often laugh loudly. Remember the old saying, "Laugh and the world laughs with you, weep and you weep alone." We are easily drawn towards happy people and tend to avoid the company of gloomy people.
4. *Happy people always count their blessings, not their failures.* They never curse their circumstances in crisis situations. If you analyse the life of any successful and happy person, you can see that he too has faced many difficult situations. Such people develop an attitude which helps them treat these situations as challenges to be overcome.
5. *Happy people are creative and thoughtful by nature.* Creativity leads to mental satisfaction and happiness, while careful planning and thinking leads to a systematic and orderly life. This will result in lesser inconvenience to themselves, as well as to others they come into contact with.
6. *Happy people are generous and considerate.* Consideration for others makes you happy and you feel good. Greed and selfishness lead to frustration and anger.

These are some of my observations about happy and successful people. They reach high positions not because of sheer luck but because of their attitude and outlook. My suggestion is that from today onwards, you too should observe and analyze their movements. I am sure that you will be convinced of what I have pointed out. Try to follow their path; Happiness and Success will be yours.

9

Emotional intelligence

> A person who is aware of the benefits of emotional intelligence would consciously react in a positive way.

Recently, I met a senior executive director of a multinational company. He has some qualities which make him very acceptable to his colleagues at different levels. This is his trump card. Having learnt that he is a very successful administrator, I asked him to reveal the secret of his success. He replied, "I think it is mainly my ability to build stress immunity. What I mean is that managing stress is my core competency. An under-standing of my own feelings, empathy for the feelings of others and the regulation of my emotions in a way that enhances my managerial ability are the main reasons for my success." I know that he is a very mature and stable person. No wonder, he is leading a very successful family life and professional life.

At the time of recruitment, most organisations lay emphasis on the candidate's I.Q. (Intelligence quotient), which is the ability to acquire academic skills and knowledge. During the early stage of one's career, one needs the ability to perform the assigned tasks in an efficient manner. This requires a higher level of I.Q. But as the person moves up the ladder, emotional skills are more critical in getting the co-operation and support of colleagues and subordinates. The term I.Q. has been a decisive criterion since the beginning of the last century. But more recently, a new measure of one's ability, which has been termed E.Q. (Emotional quotient), is gaining popularity among management experts.

The wind will be from different directions. We have to adjust our sails to meet the challenges of the wind and reach the destination.

The E.Q., being a multidimensional ability of a person, can be defined as 'the ability to command respect by building relationships' or 'the ability to get along with people and situations' or 'a positive and pro-active attitude towards all aspects of life'.

There are three essential or basic components of E.Q. The first of these, is motivating oneself. The second is motivating others and the third is empathizing with others. The first component i.e. motivating oneself, involves our own feelings and thoughts that help us to remain cool and controlled. Thus, we inspire ourselves. The other two components are interpersonal skills. One needs to synchronise one's thoughts with the other person's wavelength to ensure best results in a work situation or in personal relations.

A person who is aware of the benefits of emotional intelligence would consciously react in a positive way, to carve out the best result from any situation and eventually emerge a winner. You cannot expect that all other people will behave according to your wish. People have different temperaments. It is your ability to get along with them that helps you to become a successful person. Remember that the wind comes from different directions and we have to adjust our sails to meet the challenges of the blowing wind, and reach our destination.

10

Emotional stability

> People are very sensitive and delicate. So handle them with care.

After reading my earlier article on 'Emotional Intelligence', one of my friends said, "What you have written is absolutely correct." He added, "We cannot expect that all other people will behave according to our wish. People have varying temperaments and it is our duty to get along with them." He asked me to explain my stand a little more. When we analyze successful people, we learn that brain power, which is measured in terms of one's I.Q., is not the main criterion for success as is generally believed. In fact, it is one's character or behaviour which plays a more important role. Why are some managers more acceptable to their subordinates and colleagues than others of equal calibre? The answer is that they are well aware of the need to control their emotions. When we analyze ourselves in this context, we find that we commit mistakes or spoil relationships when we are angry or worried.

Researchers believe that anger usually arises out of a sense of being trespassed or a feeling that one is being robbed or cheated. The body's first response is a surge of energy caused by a sudden release of hormones. If a person is already under stress, the chances of hormone release are more. That is why people's temper gets frayed when they are in a fatigued or disturbed condition. If we continue to focus on the disturbing subject, our body will release more hormones. There will be a cascading effect, which makes us get even more angry. When we are in situations which provoke anger, our words and deeds develop a destructive quality. When we are calm, our reactions will be totally different. Our body needs time to process and neutralize this hormonal inbalance. For that, relaxation techniques, exercises and diverting of thoughts to other matters, will be very helpful. The good old method of counting from 10 to 1, also comes in handy.

Similarly, anxiety and worry are symptoms that the mind is preparing itself to face a difficult situation. In one sense, this experience is good to a certain extent. It helps us search efficiently for solutions to problems by focussing our mind on them. Worry is good, so long as it does not spin out of control. But excessive worry blocks the thinking process and the person becomes vulnerable to failure. Worrying unduly about failing increases the likelihood of failures. Some people are able to control this situation and come out as winners because of the self-awareness they develop over a long period. We call them mentally mature persons. They can face any difficult situation.

We come across a number of executives who are very sincere, dedicated, hardworking and result-oriented. If we promote all of them as managers purely on the basis of these qualities, we can see that in some cases their efficiency level goes down drastically. This is because they are poor in controlling their emotions. Eventually, this affects inter-personal relations. Managers with a high degree of acceptance among their subordinates and colleagues can achieve higher targets than the 'geniuses', who are stubborn 'lone elephants'. Remember that we are dealing with people. Human beings are very sensitive and delicate. So handle them with care.

11

Right attitude

> If you lose your confidence, your legs start shivering, and then the fall is certain.

Once a psychologist asked me an unusual question, "How comfortable are you in crisis situations? What is your attitude when there is a major setback in your life?" I replied: "I like crisis situations, and find it a thrilling experience to overcome them. Even if there is a major setback I never get dejected, but always keep trying until the objective is achieved." He then explained that this is the one major quality required for a successful person. In many cases, an average achiever, for one reason or another, may have a traumatic setback in life. Then he loses a large part of his confidence and self-respect and soon falls into a deep depression. This leaves the individual helpless, and in a desperate situation. He curses himself, and others label it his fate.

Traumatic setbacks may vary. Sometimes the only child in a family meets with an accident and dies, or some may lose their beloved spouse. Loss of job, failure in exams, total bankruptcy or terminal disease are, of course, not easy to accept. In all such cases, your attitude determines your future. The Law of Averages indicates that this may happen to a few people at random. Sometimes, you or I may be among them. In such situations the best course of action is to think, "This is not a new thing that has happened to me alone in this world. Many others before me have experienced the same trauma and the majority of them have already recovered from their shock. This is not the end of everything and I too will overcome this situation. Life is a mixture of sorrows and happiness." Close friends and relatives may console you in your time of grief but if you are able to console yourself, recovery will be easy and fast.

Remember that your attitude when you lose, determines how long you will take to win again. Many people take several years to fully recover from a major defeat, without realising that rational thoughts and clear thinking could have really assisted them in viewing the event from a completely different angle. For some people, a single bad experience or defeat wipes out many years of good experiences and achievements. Then they believe that their 'bad' time has started and that there is no escape from it. But they should take the view that the particular event is only an event; that it is over and cannot be undone, and they can learn from the experience for future reference. Accept the fact that the event has already taken place and that it is not the end of the world.

Life is like walking on a tight rope.

Life can be compared to 'walking on a tight rope'. For this, you need an enormous amount of mental courage to balance your body on the thin rope at high altitude. If you lose your confidence, your legs start shivering, and then the fall is certain. Here, mental strength counts much more than physical agility. An analytic assessment of the success of many personalities leads us to the irrefutable conclusion that it was their positive attitude in crisis situations and presence of mind during major setbacks that have helped them to come out in flying colours ultimately.

12

True happiness

During an interview, a journalist once asked me, "How far has wealth influenced your life?" I admit that my present financial affluence has considerably changed my life style though I come from a family with a rural background, which has its traditional simplicity. Money can buy anything that brings material comfort to our lives but happiness is derived from something else. I realise that although I can buy high quality food items and costly medicines, they need not give me good health. If I wish, I can now purchase the costliest bed in the world but there is no guarantee that it will bring me good sleep. There is a saying, 'To have sound sleep, your pillow must be filled with flowers of peace and happiness.' But as we know, peace and happiness are not things that you can directly purchase from the market. These have to spring from our inner hearts.

> Peace and happiness are not things that you can directly purchase from the market.

Comfort and happiness are totally different

I still remember the happiness and sense of elation that I felt when I purchased a second hand Lambretta scooter in 1976. At that time, I was working as a supervisor in a SSI unit manufacturing electronic equipment at Trivandrum, where I was drawing a salary of only Rs. 700/- per month. With a little money that I had saved by putting aside a few rupees every month over a period of time, and some that I had borrowed from my sister, I purchased the scooter for Rs. 2,650. Till then I was using a bicycle to go to work. I still remember the day I purchased the scooter; obviously my sense of joy and happiness was overwhelming. I used the same scooter for the next few years; I am sure that some of our staff members and managers can recall seeing it.

However, when I purchased a new Mercedes Benz car, things were totally different. The marketing executive of the company visited my office and residence several times, to persuade me to buy the car. Banks were wholeheartedly willing to give our company any amount of loan to buy it. But when I finally purchased it, having paid a hefty price of Rs. 34 lakhs, I did not experience the same thrill or enthusiasm that I had felt at the time I bought my first scooter. I learned a major lesson from this. The possession of more wealth alone is not a criterion for happiness and enthusiasm in our lives; no doubt, that is derived from something else.

I am not denying that I too seek better comfort and facilities. It is human nature, and all of us strive for it, although the level of comfort that people aspire for, may vary from person to person. I know that the pursuit of comfort is a never-ending process and it is like a mirage. Once we attain a particular level, we become disillusioned and we expect even more. But it is quite a different thing, to have peace and happiness.

13

Real success

> Doing business is like playing chess. In chess, each move is very important.

One of our associates once told me, "You have said that you always enjoy the work you are engaged in; and yet at the same time, you say that making money is not your first priority. Then what is it that really motivates you?" I replied, citing the example of an athlete who works hard and takes a lot of physical strain to win a competition. In most cases, the true value of the medal that he or she gets, does not reflect the efforts taken. So, clearly, money is not the real motivation. Now, if a budding athlete decides that he will take up sports as a career and make money from it, then I am sure that he will not excel. I believe that the top priority must be given to winning the competition or achieving something, and monetary benefits must come only second. The same applies to business also. Our top priority must be to excel in our field of operati

Doing business is like playing chess.

Doing business is like playing chess. In chess, each move is very important. Before moving one step ahead, you have to think several times and foresee the consequences. We must evaluate the impact of each move in our minds. "If I move in this direction, what would the strategy of the opponent be?" Similarly, in business, planning, calculation and foresight are all very important. Formulating different strategies and new ideas are the essence of any business. In chess also, more time is devoted to the thinking process than to the physical activity itself, which is only a simple move that takes only a second.

The roles of Chief Executives and Managers are very similar to those of chess players. They spend more time in the thinking process involved in planning, developing different strategies, forming new ideas and so on. So, in a sense, they are on duty twenty-four hours a day, and their work cannot be quantified. Even at midnight while they are asleep, they get new ideas, and sometimes these ideas may be unique. I have had a number of similar experiences in my life.

The only difference between chess and business is that in chess, the individual has to take decisions on his own whereas in business, we have a chance for group discussions and can analyse the pros and cons of a new strategy, in an open forum. Many minds work together and a foolproof new idea or strategy can emerge, which will reduce the likelihood of failure. Venturing into daring projects, having taken calculated risks, and finally seeing the light at the end of the tunnel, is a real pleasure in life. I do enjoy that kind of work. But in order to have peace of mind in our lives, we must be prepared to accept failures. Many get disheartened by setbacks, and that is the only difference between successful people and others.

14

Ignite your inner power

> The inner power in each individual is tremendous. But we are unaware of this.

I had an experience which still remains fresh in my memory. It was in the year 1979 when V-Guard had completed two years. The average production of stabilizers was then only 250 to 300 per month. I was the only sales representative of the company. There was one commission agent to book orders from the northern districts of Kerala. I used to visit the dealers once in a while to hear their grievances.

During one of those trips I was travelling by bus from Kannur to Thalassery. It was around 9.30 in the morning and I was anxious to reach the destination at the earliest. As we were passing through a village area, suddenly the bus was stopped by a few school children in the name of 'Strike'. Within no time, the road was blocked by vehicles. The students then started deflating the tyres of the vehicles one by one. I was assessing the situation. Compared to the number

of passengers, the students were fewer in number and were all in the age group of 14 to 15 years. No one was brave enough to prevent the students from damaging the tyres. Cursing themselves, the angry passengers were sitting in the bus asking questions like, "Why are the police not acting to stop this?" But the police were nowhere in sight.

When a few students came near our bus and started damaging the tyres, I mustered courage and energy and jumped out of the bus. I shouted at the top of my voice, "Don't touch the tyres. You have no right to damage the bus. If you want to demonstrate your grievance, do it in a peaceful manner. If you touch our bus, all of us will beat you and kick you out. We were also students once. This type of hooliganism cannot be tolerated. We have enough strength to drive you away." I don't know from where I got this courage. Everybody was surprised to hear my strong words.

The threat had its effect. My action inspired the majority of the passengers in the bus. They also jumped out of the bus and rounded up the boys, who were trying to deflate the tyres. The passengers became aware of their own strength and took control of the situation. They too threatened the students. Some of them went to the extent of manhandling the boys. It was with great difficulty that I managed to pacify them. Assessing the situation and sensing danger, the boys fled from the area to try their hands on another bus where there was not much resistance.

The lesson I learnt from this episode is about 'mass psychology.' Most of the people in any group will be passive. Someone has to take the initiative to inspire them. Individuals have their abilities but a leader must be there to initiate action. If we are fighting for a good cause, we will definitely get a lot of support. The internal power in each individual is tremendous. But we are unaware of this.

15

Be fair and firm

> If we are firm in our decisions, we can overcome any type of hurdles.

A friend of mine asked me a very valid question, "I will be fair in my dealings. But what will I do if somebody misbehaves or is unfair to me?" My answer was, "If you are fair in your dealings and yet if somebody is unfair to you, then you must be firm." If we are firm in our decisions, we can overcome any type of hurdles and many of the so called 'tigers' will turn out to be but 'paper tigers.' This reminds me of a story which was told by one of my professors while I was in college. He was emphasizing the importance of self-confidence, firmness in decisions, and challenging unfair deeds which should be cultivated in all students, who are the future citizens of the country.

The story goes like this. In a crowded bazaar area, full of shops, an antisocial person used to come every evening with a knife. The public knew him, a notorious criminal in the locality who had killed two persons and had been to jail several times. He used to threaten the shopkeepers brandishing his shining knife. He found that no one had the courage to question him. Uttering nasty words he used to frighten the shopkeepers and demand money. To avoid confrontation they used to give him five or ten rupees. They were afraid to lodge a complaint with the police because that could spark off personal vengeance. In this way he would collect Rs. 50 to Rs. 75 everyday, enough to spend in a liquor shop. This drama repeated everyday and he was in a position to collect the same amount from some other shopkeepers on a rotation basis.

One day, one of the shopkeepers became sick and his son, who had just completed his college studies, took charge of the shop. As usual, the criminal came to the shop shouting filthy words. The youngster, shocked by the abusive words, wanted to react. But a senior accountant pacified him saying, "Your father used to give him five rupees. Don't try to provoke him". Much against his will, the youngster reluctantly gave the rowdy five rupees. But he could not sleep that night. He went on thinking, "Is this fair? Why has nobody come forward to stop this exploitation? Is there any solution for this?" Can you think of one!

16

Truth begets courage

> Leaders and heroes are creating history out of adverse conditions.

The next day, our youngster was totally disturbed and was in search of a solution to the problem. In the afternoon, he planned something and was ready for action. Everyone could see the determination on his face. That evening, the rowdy came as usual uttering nasty words and challenging people with the knife. As he was coming from one end of the road, our youngster jumped onto the road and raised a knife challenging, "Who is brave enough to face this knife?!!" People were really frightened as the rowdy and the youngster moved towards each other from the two ends of the road. They came closer and closer and nobody dared to stop them. Shopkeepers lowered their shutters to avoid watching the bloodshed. Many of them peeped through the windows to know the final outcome.

I know you are also eager to know what happened. Aren't you? The rowdy was a cunning fellow. He assessed the situation and changed his tactics. When the youngster came closer, the rowdy hugged him. Pretending that they were friends, he challenged all the other shopkeepers, "Who is brave enough to fight against these two knives?" Suddenly, he vanished from the scene. People came out and started praising the youngster as a hero. He really deserved the praise. The shopkeepers were thus freed from the terror and exploitation of the rowdy. Thereafter the rowdy was not seen in the bazaar area. After a few days, he appeared in another bazaar in a nearby town using the same tactics.

The strong message of this story is that if you are on the right track and if there is strong determination, you need not fear anything. Success is reserved for brave and straightforward people. Muscle power, money power or luck plays only a minor role in this process. Leaders and heroes are creating history out of adverse conditions. You need not spend too much time in search of a leader of that kind. Our own Father of the Nation, Mahatma Gandhi is a great example. He never applied any muscle power or money power. His only asset was his will power. We all know the rest of the story.

Three English proverbs throw light on this point:

1. Success often goes to those who dare and act. It seldom goes to the timid.
2. Sweet are the uses of adversities.
3. If there is a will, there is a way.

17

Nobody can make you inferior without your consent

> Everything depends upon our attitude.

It is a parent's duty to motivate his or her children and help them discover their hidden talents. You can inspire them with words like, "You are intelligent and capable" or, "You have a lot of talent but you have to work hard."

We generally tend to compare our children with others, though with the best of intentions. But such comparisons usually irritate children and yield negative results.

You may probably think that you would have done better in life if your parents were aware of child psychology while you were young. There again, I have a difference of opinion. Many people have come

up in life without either the support of their parents or an affluent family background. Everything depends on our attitude.

I know of two brothers whose father was a complete drunkard. This man ruined his health, squandered his wealth and died leaving the burden of a huge debt on his family. The two brothers are now grown up. The elder brother now holds a very high position in a multinational company. He is a very systematic, punctual and disciplined person. He has never touched alcohol.

When I asked him the secret of his success in life, he said, "My father was an alcohol addict who ruined everything. So I decided not to follow the path of my father. I worked hard and have finally reached this position."

On the other hand, the younger brother turned out to be a drifter who was always drunk. He could not hold on to any job. He also neglected his family. When anyone tried to advise him, his stock reply was, "I learnt this habit from my father." This is only a lame excuse. I strongly believe that everything depends upon our own attitude. For our failures and incompetence we can find any number of excuses.

For our failures and incompetence we can find any number of excuses.

I still remember a beautiful and meaningful sentence I once came across, 'Nobody can make you inferior without your consent.' If you allow yourself to be overwhelmed by negative feelings such as, "I am not capable; I am not intelligent; I am not well qualified; I am not healthy; I am not beautiful or I am not wealthy enough," you are bound to develop an inferiority complex, which will cripple your real talents. Instead, think about people who have come up in life despite many disadvantages. That will give you enough courage to perform better in life.

So, ultimately, everything depends on your attitude. We are the creators of our own destiny.

18

Forgive and forget

> Forget what you have lost so that you can achieve what still remains.

24th August, 2000 was a black letter day in the history of V-Guard. The godown at our Hyderabad branch was affected by the floods in the region. As a result, thousands of stabilizers and other products were damaged. The estimated loss was between 30 to 40 lakh rupees. There was no insurance cover against flood damages. Some of my friends and relatives were reluctant to contact me on the phone because they were under the impression that I was in deep distress, and they were wondering how they could console me. But those who know me well, know that I always maintain a calm and cool frame of mind. I am a person who is not easily disturbed by crisis situations.

I developed this attitude as a result of attending various training programmes and reading many books on this topic. In order to avoid worry and to be happy, the first lesson we have to learn is: 'Forget what you have lost so that you can achieve what still remains.' In many ways, happiness is a personal matter. There are three things to remember about happiness: *1. Happiness is important 2. Happiness is desirable 3. Happiness is possible.*

Abraham Lincoln once said, "Most people are about as happy as they make up their mind to be." Happiness is a state of mind. It is you, and you alone who decides whether you shall be happy or unhappy. It is usually believed that only those who have money, power, position and fame can be really happy. That is totally wrong. There are several people who, in spite of having achieved all these things, end up in misery.

There is a saying, 'Even the costliest bed cannot offer you deep sleep unless your mind is calm and peaceful.' Many rich people need sleeping pills daily. On the other hand, even a physically disabled or a financially weak person can be happy inspite of his/her drawbacks. So everything depends on your mental attitude.

"Don't carry your mistakes (and others' too) in your heart for too long." Otherwise, you cannot be happy in life. So, 'forgive and forget' is not merely broad-mindedness. It is essential for your own mental peace. We must learn to find happiness within ourselves. Happiness is an intrinsic state. 'Happiness is earned, not got'. It cannot be found outside. It may sound shocking but it is true. By anticipating and accepting the worst, we have nothing to lose. Remember, all days may not be alike and we have to accept them wholeheartedly. We must also remember that there is no point in crying over spilt milk. If we imbibe these principles and put them into practice, we can be happy in life.

19

Analyse the effectiveness of each work

> Every individual should apply his or her mind to analyse the effectiveness of each piece of work.

After the process of globalization and liberalization began in India, we have seen cut-throat competition everywhere. As a result, the survival of many industries is at stake. In fact, even V-Guard has started feeling the pinch. Our turnover could not be raised to the expected level. Senior Managers met urgently to chalk out ways to reduce the cost of production in order to bring the situation under control. Until this financial year (2000-2001), V-Guard had been doing consistently well. It is high time now to think seriously about innovative ideas, cost reduction, effectiveness, efficiency and other similar factors.

Over a period of time, any organisation develops a particular work culture and system and starts moving in a set pattern. Many stereotyped tasks become part of our routine job. Eventually, we forget to analyze the real need or relevance of a particular work. The general attitude seems to be: "I am just following what my predecessor used to do."

This reminds me of a story about a *Sanyasi* who had a number of disciples. Every morning this *Guruji* preached to his disciples under the shade of a tree near the ashram. During this time, a cat used to come and roam around the disciples as a nuisance. Naturally, it distracted the attention of the disciples. To prevent this, the *Guruji* asked them to tie up the cat. As this practice went on for a few days, the disciples started tying up the cat without waiting for the *Guruji's* order.

This practice continued for years, even after the Guruji died and a senior disciple took up the role of preaching. One day the cat died. The next morning before the preaching started, the new Guruji said, "From the days of our beloved Guruji, we have been following the practice of tying up a cat before the preaching started. Now that the

cat is dead, please find a new cat to tie up before the preaching starts. Let us continue the system introduced by our Guruji."

The moral of the story is that, if we analyze our day-to-day routine work, we will find many non-relevant and unproductive activities. Every individual should apply his or her mind to analyse the effectiveness of each piece of work. This is applicable to all the avenues like design, procurement of raw materials, production, packing, transporting, advertisement, marketing, after-sale service, accounts, electronic data processing and human resource development. Always ask yourself the question, "Is there a better way to do the same job?", or to be more specific, "Is there any alternative to a particular component?" We can do wonders if we practise this sincerely in our respective jobs.

20
Be inquisitive

"I keep six honest serving men
They taught me all I know;
Their names are
What and Why and When
And Where and How and Who"

We must always be inquisitive. This is the only way we can improve ourselves.

Have you heard of, or read this poem? It was written by Rudyard Kipling, a famous British writer, who won the Nobel Prize. In a nutshell, it means that we can improve our knowledge only by asking questions.

You may have noticed that many people are reluctant to ask questions and acquire knowledge. Some of them probably think, "If I ask that particular question, I may look foolish or ignorant in the eyes of the other person, who may think that I have asked a silly question." But the fact is, that we must always be inquisitive. This is the only way we can improve ourselves. If we go around pretending, "I know everything", we cannot acquire more knowledge. The first step towards the acquisition of knowledge, is to ask questions. In fact, the admission of our ignorance is the first step to progress.

Kids always ask questions, even silly ones, without any inhibition. We must have the same attitude if we are to make progress. All of us know that Thomas Alva Edison was a great scientist, who invented many things. But as a student at school, he was rated below average. He had a peculiar disability in writing and pronunciation, which is known as Dyslexia. He was a very inquisitive boy, who would always ask his teachers and parents many questions. They were invariably not in a position to clear out many of his doubts. They even thought that he was fooling them by asking such questions. Because of this writing disability he could not score even the minimum marks in the examinations.

Finally, he was thrown out of his school. After that, he never attended any school or college!! His father also was fed up with the boy. But his mother identified the latent genius in him and started teaching him. She referred many books and sought the help of experts to answer his inquisitive questions. History reveals that Edison's mother played a major role in developing his scientific talents.

The electric bulb is just one of his many inventions. He noticed that if electricity is passed through a thin metal filament, it emits light. We may think that many inventions were made by accident and sheer luck. Certainly not! Inquisitiveness and perseverance are the two major factors behind every achievement. He tried the use of many alloys to make a suitable bulb filament. Many of them gave very feeble light and some fused within seconds. But the search continued. History reveals that he tried more than 250 alloys before declaring that electricity can be used for lighting purposes.

Many of us normally give up trying, after one or two failures or when there are obstacles. Edison teaches us, "Be inquisitive; never give up halfway; try again and again." In this context, I am happy to say that the V-Guard group has picked up momentum, thanks to our sustained efforts with focus on cost control and innovations. Never give up. Be inquisitive and persevering. We can do wonders.

21

Your personality is reflected in your deeds

> It is education and experience, combined with an attitudinal change, that makes people more humble and noble.

Long ago, an old 'Maharishi' was meditating under a banyan tree. He was blind. A man came up to him and asked in a harsh tone. "Hey old man, did you hear anyone passing this way?" The sage replied, "No, my good man, I did not hear anyone."

After a while, another man came by and asked, "Sir, did you hear anyone going this way?" The Sanyasi replied. "Oh yes, a man passed by only just now, and asked me the same question." The man went away.

After some time, yet another man came by and asked him, "Respected sir, sorry for interrupting your meditation. Have you heard anyone passing this way?" The old sage replied, "Yes, your Majesty. A soldier came first. Then your minister. Both of them asked me the same question."

This reply took the new visitor by surprise. He asked, "Respected sir, how do you know that I am a king and that the other two were a soldier and a minister? You are blind. Have you acquired a sixth sense through your meditation?" The sage replied, "No, Your Majesty, I am just a poor Sanyasi. I have no divine powers. I could identify them by the manner in which they spoke. The first man spoke very rudely, addressing me as 'Old Man'. The second one was a little more polite, addressing me as 'Sir'. But Your Majesty was the most polite, addressing me as 'Respected sir' and apologizing for interrupting my meditation." The King went away, astonished by the old sage's common sense.

We must have come across many such situations in our own lives. Yes, we can assess people by the manner of their speaking. We need not have any extra intelligence to assess people from their behaviour. One's personality is reflected in one's words and deeds. If someone is basically arrogant and rude, the public will easily understand his real nature, even if he pretends to be noble and polite. We cannot hide many things from a large group of people for a long time.

Naturally, noble and polite people will have more followers. In English, there is a proverb, 'Empty vessels make the most noise.' Its Malayalam equivalent is: 'നിറകുടം തുളുമ്പില്ല,' which means, 'If a pot is full to the brim, it will not spill over.' If we are really aware of our weaknesses, we will surely become more polite in our manners. It is education and experience, combined with an attitudinal change, that makes people more humble and noble. In an organisation, subordinates look for such qualities in their superiors and always prefer noble and polite people as their leaders.

22

Rule over challenge and controversy

The crucial decisions taken by a person during crisis situations determine his growth or decline in life.

'The ultimate measure of a man is not where he stands in moments of comfort and convenience, but where he stands at times of challenge and controversy.' These are the words of the great social reformer Martin Luther King. It is quite true that only in difficult situations we can really judge the leadership qualities of a man. The crucial decisions taken by a person during crisis situations determine his growth or decline in life.

Successful people, after achieving one goal, set for themselves a slightly bigger target, follow the established and tested route to success and come up with new achievements. With the experience of fulfilled

Ships are safer in the harbour but they are not meant for being kept at rest.

dreams, these people latch onto fresh dreams, bigger challenges and more exciting objectives. Thus they enjoy continuous excitement in living, working and winning. In between, there may be some failures. But their policy is to keep trying and there is no let-up in their enthusiasm. Their life gets constantly renewed by exciting experience. They are always happy, eager and creative.

Successful people find happiness in striving for new goals rather than in being content with the fruits of attained objectives. They are always eager to pursue new goals in a competitive and innovative spirit. Happiness comes to those who never lose the excitement of going after new goals. For them, the thirst for achieving something better, is a way of life.

Successful and dynamic people know that '*ships are safer in the harbour but that is not what they are meant for.*' Only when they cruise on the high seas, do they face stormy weather and rough seas, before reaching their destination. Similarly, a soldier has no chance of winning medals till he goes to the battlefield because that is where he is supposed to be. If he just sits back, his bravery and strength will never come to light.

Friends, only when one takes the risk of getting a few scars does one gain the opportunity of winning stars. If we analyse the lifestyle of successful persons, we can clearly see that risk taking and hard work are the main contributory factors of their success.

23

Trust, to get the best

> Subordinates will do their best if they are convinced that you have trust in them.

We regularly advertise and project a slogan, "V-Guard, the name you can trust." Normally a brand name gets popular because customers develop a trust in the products, based on their experience. Contrary to popular belief, brand names do not gain acceptance from heavy advertisements. I strongly believe that the number of satisfied customers determines the popularity of a brand name. A satisfied customer is an eloquent ambassador of a product. If he is happy with the performance of the product he has bought, he will share his joy with his friends and relatives. This type of experience-sharing is ten times more effective than advertising on TV channels or newspapers.

When a sale takes place, there is an element of trust in that particular transaction. The customer believes that the product is worth the money he pays for it and he expects a certain level of quality and

after-sale service. A common rule is: 'If you trust me, I cannot let you down.' A customer buys something from a company because of his trust and the company has the responsibility not to let the customer down.

The same principle is applicable to leaders too. We follow someone we can trust and a true leader honours that trust. A leader must have consistent value systems. When we search for names of great leaders, the first name that comes to our mind is Mahatma Gandhi. Because of his self-discipline, patience and clarity of thinking, he could attract a large number of followers. Leaders must trust and accept the people they lead. Such acceptance requires tolerance of imperfection. Anybody can lead perfect people. But a group of people will differ in attitudes and calibre. We cannot expect all of them to be one hundred percent perfect. Many of them must be having different types of weaknesses. A true leader must have the patience and willingness to absorb their weaknesses and guide them in the proper direction. The basic principle 'If you trust me, I cannot let your down' works both ways. People will do their best to live up to your trust in them. In such cases, people are ready even to die for the sake of their leaders.

The observations made above hold good and valid in the making of an effective, successful manager too. Subordinates will do their best if they are convinced that you have trust in them. Self-discipline, patience, clarity of thinking and affection towards subordinates make a manager more effective in his profession. Whether it relates to a product, an organisation or a manager, it is essential that we have to gain the trust of others to ensure success.

24

Live in the present

> Courageous people never worry about their work load.

Once upon a time, there was an old clock manufacturer who made winding clocks. He used to fabricate the inner machinery of a clock and place it in an artistically crafted and beautiful cabinet. One day, after completing the work, he said to the clock, "Look, I have completed all the work and you are ready to function. When I wind the spring, you will have to tick two times in one second (winding clocks usually tick twice a second) non-stop at least for 50 years." The manufacturer wound the clock spring, started the pendulum, and the clock started functioning.

After a few minutes, the new clock started to think, "I have to work for 50 years non-stop ticking twice a second. That means 120 ticks in a minute, 7200 ticks in an hour and 1,72,800 ticks in a day. For 365 days in an year, there will have to be 6,30,72,000 ticks and for 50 years, my God, it will be 315 crore ticks!!" A kind of nervousness crept into various parts of the new clock. It could not move its parts. Overwhelmed by the thought of the task ahead, the clock suddenly stopped functioning. The manufacturer checked all the parts. Since there was no fault in the machinery, he started the clock once again. After the clock worked fine for a few minutes, the thought of having to tick 315 crore times returned to its mind and the clock stopped functioning once again.

A grandfather clock in the same room was observing what was going on and it wanted to know what the problem was. After listening to the young clock it said, "Look, I am 68 years old and have been functioning smoothly till now. Lakhs of clocks are working all over the world without any interruption. Why can't you do the same? Don't worry about the future. Just perform today's duties and forget about tomorrow." These wise words were an eye-opener to the new clock, which resumed its assigned duty of ticking twice a second without worrying about the future.

The moral of the story is very clear. Some people never venture into any new assignments simply anticipating failures. They spend a great deal of time just thinking about what lies ahead and try to find all the negative aspects of the project. As a result, they never manage to start any new venture. If we focus on negative aspects, we can find a hundred reasons for not doing a task. Simply worrying about the future will take you nowhere. Courageous people never worry about their workload. This is the basic difference between successful people and others. Problems will be there in everyone's life. But merely anticipating problems and not doing anything are the characteristics of lazy people. Instead of being overwhelmed by the enormity of a task, our attitude should be, "There will be problems and I will face them then and there." If you religiously follow this principle, success will definitely be yours.

25

Realise your strength

A willingness to accept challenges and the ability to handle crisis situations in the proper way, make people successful.

After reading my previous article, some of our managers took care to cultivate the habit of not worrying about tomorrow. Anticipating failures, many people shun new tasks. They don't remember the fact that the journey of a thousand miles begins with a 'single step'. But it is part of human nature to worry about the future. That is why all religions lay emphasis on not worrying about tomorrow. The Bible says, "Look at the birds in the sky. They never store any food in a godown for the future. Yet they survive. See the flowers in the field. They never weave any clothes. Yet they are beautiful. So don't worry about the future." The Bhagvad Gita says, "You have the right only to work. Never expect the fruits of your efforts. They will reach you in their own way." Some of my

Hiding away from realities leads to disaster.

Muslim friends say that there are similar exhortations in the Quran also. All these indicate that human beings have always worried about the future.

When we analyse the lives of people who changed the course of history, we realize that it is their attitude and will power which were their main strengths. For example, even though he knew that it was going to be an uphill task, Mahatma Gandhi plunged into the freedom struggle. In the early days of the movement the British rulers miserably failed in assessing his strength. They contemptuously referred to him as a 'half-naked fakir (sanyasi)'. We all know the rest of the story. A willingness to accept challenges and the ability to handle crisis situations in the proper way make people successful. Those who have these qualities know that failures are the stepping stones to success. They learn and accept many lessons from failures.

When we went to Kenya on a wildlife safari, besides many animals, we saw a rare bird, the ostrich, in large numbers. As we all know, ostriches are the biggest birds on earth, weighing around 200-350 kg. each. During the journey, our guide who drove us through the wildlife sanctuary, explained to us that ostriches can run at a speed of 64 km per hour and can cover several kilometres at a stretch. However, in crisis situations, for example when chased by a lion or tiger, they lose confidence, stop running and bury their heads in the sand in fear, believing that they were safely hiding from the chasing enemy. We can imagine their fate! Hiding or running away from realities leads to disaster.

How can we cultivate the courage to face crisis situations? We can do it best by reading inspiring articles about successful people and by observing how effective and efficient managers function. If we make a determined attempt, we too can develop self-confidence.

26

Perseverance can make wonders happen

> Have a burning desire to realize your goals. Success will be yours.

An eight-year old girl heard her parents talking about her little brother. All she knew was that he was very sick and that her parents did not have enough money to treat him. Only a very expensive surgery could save him and no one was willing to lend them the money. One night, she heard her daddy telling her tearful mother in desperation, "Only a miracle can save him now." She could not sleep that night.

She used to keep coins she got as pocket money in a small box. She poured out all the coins on a table and counted carefully. The next day, she held the box tightly and went to a nearby medical store. She poured out all the coins on the glass counter and told the pharmacist, "My little brother is very sick and I want to buy a miracle for him." "What miracle?" the pharmacist was confused. He had never heard

"I want to buy a miracle. How much does a miracle cost?"

of a tablet or syrup called 'miracle'. "My brother has something bad growing inside his head and my daddy says that only 'a miracle' can save him," she explained and asked, "How much does a miracle cost?" The pharmacist smiled sadly and told the girl, "I am sorry, we don't sell miracles here."

A well-dressed customer who observed what was going on asked the little girl, "What kind of miracle does your brother need?" "I don't know," she replied with tears in her eyes. "He is seriously ill and mummy says he needs an operation. My daddy can't pay for it. So I have brought all my savings", she said. The man asked her how much she had and she replied that she had one dollar and eleven cents. Then he said, "Give me the money and take me to your brother and parents. Let me see if I have the kind of miracle you need."

I read this in a book on management. But this is not an imaginary story. It really happened. The well-dressed man was Dr. Carlton Armstrong, a famous surgeon in the US, who had specialised in neurosurgery. The operation was conducted free of cost and it was a success. The boy was brought back to normal life. "That surgery was a real miracle. I wonder how much it would have cost," his mother said. The little girl smiled. She knew exactly how much the miracle had cost – one dollar and eleven cents, plus the burning wish of a loving sister. Perseverance can make miracles happen. That is what the story tells us.

I found this real-life story to be very touching. I have quoted this in many forums. I learnt a great lesson from this. To achieve any target we must have a burning desire like that of the girl. If we have a persistent attitude towards solving a problem, a solution will emerge from somewhere. But we must have the perseverance first. Have a burning desire to realize your goals. Success will be yours.

27

Pygmalion effect

> If we have the urge for perfection, hard work and a burning desire, we can work wonders in this world.

In the previous article, we looked at the importance of having a burning desire and the need for perseverance in the pursuit of one's goals. There is yet another story which lays emphasis on the same subject. This is drawn from Greek mythology and it is about the creation of a statue. In ancient Greece there was a sculptor called Pygmalion, who could carve beautiful statues of Greek goddesses and gods. The public admired the wonderful creations of Pygmalion. The statues were crafted with such perfection that many wondered whether there was life in them. One day, this bachelor sculptor decided to carve the statue of a woman, in marble. He was determined to make it the most beautiful statue he had ever made, his masterpiece.

He started his work, toiling through day and night and spent hours together to give perfection to his statue. Even after the completion of the statue, he spent hours everyday polishing it and giving the final touches. The statue of a young beautiful woman with a smiling face was the net result of his long, painstaking effort. He named it 'Galathea'. He was so impressed with the statue that he gradually began to fall in love with the marble piece. He adorned it with gold ornaments and clothed it in fine raiments.

A burning desire grew within Pygmalion, and he wished that the statue were alive, so that he could marry her. He started praying to 'Aphrodite' who is the goddess of love in Greek mythology (corresponding to 'Kama Devan' in Hindu mythology). He prayed so

Management experts have started using a term "Pygmalion effect".

ardently and his desire was so strong that finally, Aphrodite was pleased and granted him his wish. One morning, Pygmalion was praying to the goddess of love, before the statue. He could not believe his eyes when the eyelids of the statue fluttered and the fingertips moved! Galathea stepped down from the platform and reached out to him. The story ends with their marriage and they lived happily ever after.

Here we can see the effect of three factors 1.) The urge for perfection 2.) Hard work, and 3.) A burning desire. If we have these three qualities we can work wonders in this world. Management experts have started using the term, 'Pygmalion effect', which means that if we have a strong desire like that of Pygmalion, we can achieve unbelievable goals. When we analyse the characters of successful people, inventors or great artists, we find these qualities inherent in them. To achieve a great goal, it may take months or years. There will be a number of stumbling blocks on the way. Many people show a great deal of enthusiasm initially, but instead of persisting in their objectives, some of them give up halfway. I strongly believe that the creation of Veega Land (Now re-named Wonderla, Kochi) is the result of the 'Pygmalion effect'.

28

Integrated success formula

> The fast and consistent will always beat the slow and steady.

All of us must have heard many times the story of the hare and the tortoise, who bet on a race, which the tortoise eventually won, simply because the hare was overconfident. The hare ran briskly for a while, but when he saw that he was far ahead of the tortoise, he decided that it was safe to rest under a tree for some time before continuing the race. However, he soon fell asleep. Even though the tortoise was slow, he worked hard and plodded along steadily without a break. He soon overtook the hare and won the race. When the hare woke up, he realized that he had lost the race. As we all know, the moral of the story is, 'Slow and steady wins the race'.

As I said earlier, this is a story we have all heard in our childhood, and my father, who is now eighty-seven, recalls hearing the same story even during his childhood. So presumably, it could date back to the 19th Century or even earlier. But I read a new version of this old story in V & We which is perhaps more relevant to the 21st century, characterized by liberalization and globalization, which have transformed the global economy. Let me repeat the story here once again. The hare was disheartered for a while for having lost the race, but he did some introspection. After some soul-searching, he realised that he had lost the race only because he had been overconfident, careless and proud. If he had not taken things for granted, there was no chance for the tortoise to beat him. So he challenged the tortoise to another race. The tortoise agreed. This time, the hare went all out

It is good to be slow and steady, but it is always better to be fast and reliable.

and ran without stopping, from start to finish, and won by several kilometres. So the moral of the story here is, 'The fast and consistent can always beat the slow and steady.' If we consider two types of people, one slow, methodical and reliable, and the other fast, still reliable and consistent, then the latter will achieve more targets than the slow methodical person. It is good to be slow and steady but it is always better to be fast and reliable.

In this era of globalization, when rapid changes are taking place in the world, 'Survival of the fittest' is the order of the day. The good old proverb, 'The early bird gets the worm' is more meaningful in this new century. In many cases, people who are fast, are generally not consistent. If they can strive to become more methodical and reliable, then the results will be astonishing. Similarly, if slow coaches can become faster and more aggressive, they can also achieve higher and higher targets.

29

People manager

> The ability to maintain good human relations is an essential art, which has to be developed, if one is to become a good manager.

It is not essential for a good artist or a sculptor to know anything about the intricacies of human relations in order to assume leadership positions in their respective professions. This is also probably the case, with an orthopaedic surgeon or a scientist in a research institute. In such cases, what is essential for success is their proficiency in the subject and an inclination to work hard. On the other hand, the ability to deal with people, is the first and foremost skill required by anyone aspiring to be an outstanding manager. Acceptance, both by subordinates and colleagues, are very important when we judge a Manager.

The ability to maintain good human relations is an essential art, which has to be developed, if one is to become a good manager. Since the main duty of a manager or a leader is to deal with people, he will need to develop the art of maintaining good human relations. Remember, he will frequently need to deal with a wide variety of people such as customers, dealers, raw material suppliers, staff members, bureaucrats and so on. Their acceptance makes him/her an outstanding manager. Some managers fail in this aspect even though they may be intelligent and hardworking. A leader must be capable of judging correctly the strengths and weaknesses of his subordinates, and be able to direct and motivate them. A real leader will create a conducive atmosphere in the organisation so that the abilities of the junior staff will flourish and the organisation will get young and capable managers.

A successful manager should have the ability to deal with a wide variety of people.

The real duty of a sincere leader is not only to discover the talents of his subordinates but also to groom them to become good managers. This requires a lot of patience and meticulous attention. Some managers are fond of saying that it is easier to complete a task themselves rather than delegating it to their juniors and monitoring them closely. I agree that delegating a task and giving proper guidance is a time-consuming affair.

However, one of the main lessons I have learned from my varied experience over the years, is that when delegating tasks, one should never expect a hundred percent perfection in the results. Everyone has his own way of completing a task, which sometimes may not measure up to our expectations or preferences. Yet, we can closely watch their progress and give directions. One has to give a lot of freedom to the juniors to complete their tasks. We must have the generosity to appreciate their success. Let their success be the monuments to your leadership abilities.

30

Education – the parrot's way!

> We force our children to memorise what is written in their textbooks.

In 1994, I attended a two-week management training programme in Japan arranged by an organisation called AOTS (Association for Overseas Technical Scholarship). Most of the faculty members were professors from different universities providing consultancy services to leading companies like Sony, Toshiba, Toyota, etc.

One of them had been to India several times on behalf of many multinational companies to study the business and the market potential here. He had an in-depth knowledge about our education system at both the school and university levels. According to him, schools and universities in India do not lay enough stress on the development of the creative faculty or innovative thinking among students.

On the other hand, in Japan the curriculum and syllabus are designed to bring out the real talents of every child. Besides, many exercises and project works are given at the school and college levels to develop their creativity and innovative skills. Moreover, university professors and students are engaged in research and development work for industries on a contract basis.

The scenario in India is quite different. We force our children to memorize what is written in their textbooks. A student who can memorize his lessons, gets the first rank, even without grasping the real meaning or implications of what he has studied! In Malayalam, there is a saying, 'തത്തമ്മേ പൂച്ച പൂച്ച' which means, 'Parrot, beware: the cat is there.' The point here is that if you teach a parrot a few words, it will simply repeat them without understanding the exact meaning of the words.

I heard this old saying very often in my childhood days from my teachers, who were trying to illustrate that there was no point in just memorizing things without knowing their real meaning. But the teachers made no attempt to explain concepts or principles with illustrations. Obviously, they were not even trained for that. They were also not even in a position to explain how or why this old saying, 'തത്തമ്മേ പൂച്ച പൂച്ച' came into existence.

Inquisitive by nature, I tried to trace the origin of this old saying and made up a story to explain it. It goes like this: Once upon a time,

in a village there was a farmer. His son had a pet parrot. It used to repeat any sound the boy made. He also had a cat which would try to attack the parrot though it was in a cage. One day when the cat was not around, the boy said, 'തത്തമ്മേ പൂച്ച പൂച്ച' just to tease the parrot. Since the parrot did not know the real meaning of those words, it simply repeated them in a pleasant tone. Otherwise, the parrot would have been too scared to repeat them. The story has a moral and contains a message for all of us.

If the teachers narrate some examples to illustrate a difficult theorem in mathematics or science, the students can grasp its real meaning without much difficulty. It then becomes easy for them to memorize the lesson with a clear understanding of its meaning. The net result is that students will find their subjects more interesting. This will lead to a better learning experience, more creativity and innovative thinking.

31

Evils of unbridled freedom

> One has to undergo a three to six months' training programme to become a taxi or bus driver.

Some time back, I had visited Germany, France and Australia. While travelling through these developed countries, one major difference I noticed was the civic sense of the people. I was struck by their attitude of 'causing less inconvenience to others.' Perhaps, the most striking example of this attitude is their discipline in obeying traffic rules. At traffic junctions, when the traffic lights switch to yellow, after the green signal, all motorists will slow down their vehicles and prepare to come to a halt, even before the red light comes on. On the other hand, in our country we accelerate when we see that the lights have switched to yellow; in fact, some people never stop even if they see a red light.

In those countries, the horn is used as a last resort, and we don't hear the sound of horns even on a busy street, full of vehicles, except in rare cases. Sounding the horn is considered equivalent to scolding or shouting at the driver of the vehicle just in front of you. When I purchased a Benz car, one thing I noticed was that the horn sounded very weak. I asked the service engineer, "Even after paying such a high price for this expensive car, why can't they fit a good horn?" He replied that in developed countries they seldom sound the horn except in emergencies, and that they preferred horns which sound pleasant and soft. But in our country we compete with each other to install the most powerful horns available in the market.

Similarly, using a mobile phone while driving is a serious offence in all developed countries, whereas such a practice is seen as a status symbol in our country.

Remember, we too have the same rules but we take pleasure in violating them! In those countries pedestrians are given the highest priority on the roads. Even if someone crosses the road without obeying the traffic signals, it is the duty of the motorists to stop their vehicles and allow him to cross. In all developed countries one has to undergo a three to six months' training programme to become a taxi or bus driver. The training focusses on how to behave politely with customers, the importance of traffic rules, and so on. Here, in our country since the drivers of public service vehicles do not get such training, they are often a nightmare to tourists and on the roads.

Using mobile phone while driving is a status symbol in our country.

Another thing I noticed there was that the law is enforced very strictly without fear or favour. Furthermore, the officials are not corrupt. If you are found guilty of a traffic offence, your licence will be detained for six months, one year or two years, depending on the gravity of the offence, and in the case of accidents that result in death, you will be put in jail, just as you would be, for any other criminal offence. So, it is clear that we certainly enjoy excessive freedom in our own country!

32

Shame, shame!

> We are compelled to remain silent and not to reveal the truth about those in power.

Due to many reasons, it is often not advisable for industrialists to respond or react to many social evils. A friend of mine felt that criticising union leaders would hinder the growth of our business. This reminds me of a story about a king who never bothered about what people said.

One day, the king left the castle and went out into the streets wearing his crown and carrying the sceptre in hand. But to everyone's surprise, he was not wearing any clothes except a loincloth. The people were aware that it was dangerous to criticise their king. So everybody began praising him saying, "My Lord, your clothes are beautiful." Another said, "You look very handsome in these nice clothes." Yet another pointed out, "The jewels in your crown are glittering." Nobody was brave enough to point out that the King was without clothes. They knew that if they revealed the truth, the consequences would be severe.

But seeing the drama one five-year-old child openly and loudly exclaimed, "Shame, Shame. Puppy Shame! Our King is naked!" Hearing this, the panicked elders warned the kid, "Don't repeat this; or else, you will be punished."

This is a simple story. But similar incidents are occurring around us in our day-to-day life. However, our lips are often sealed. We are compelled to remain silent and not to reveal the truth about those in power. No one wants to take the risk of criticising the rulers.

All of us know that Kerala is an industrially backward area. Everyone knows the reasons for this. Although the State Government is trying its best to invite industrialists from North India and abroad to set up industrial units in Kerala, their efforts don't succeed.

33

Survival of the fittest

Unless you have enough self-confidence, it is very difficult to succeed in life.

Recently, I happened to listen to an old Malayalam song. The meaning conveyed by the lines was: 'As long as you are happy and prospering, there will be thousands of people to join you. But when you are in trouble, only your shadow will be there to keep you company.'

There is an important message in these words, which tells us that we shall be alone during crisis situations and to expect wholehearted support from others, is mere foolishness. You may have experienced this in your own lives on some occasions. We cannot blame others for this because they too are struggling for survival in their own way in this highly competitive world. Your problems are of only secondary importance to them.

This is where your self-confidence comes into play. Whether you are a manager, clerk, student or anyone else for that matter, unless you have enough self-confidence, it is very difficult to succeed in life. History clearly reveals that only those who had ample self-confidence could come up in life, overcoming adverse situations. If someone strongly feels that he is unlucky, he will not be in a position to find a solution to any problem.

On the other hand, people with confidence in themselves always succeed in overcoming hurdles. So it is our own attitude or mindset which makes all the difference.

During your school days, you might have noticed that your classmates with self-confidence always did better than others by scoring more marks in exams or making great achievements in sports and arts. Because of fear, some students cannot perform well in exams and competitions even though they have a sound knowledge of the subjects they study.

Self-reliance is another vital ingredient of success. In Malayalam, there is a proverb which says, 'തനിക്കു താനും, പുരയ്ക്ക് തൂണും.' This means that 'Just as a building depends on its pillars to remain stable, you have only yourself to depend upon and not anybody else.' There is a risk in relying too much on others since your success will then depend entirely on others' co-operation. I certainly agree that since we are all social beings, mutual help has a significant role in society. But a close study of successful people reveals that all of them demonstrate a high degree of independence in their attitudes.

Another proverb in Malayalam states: 'If you do not sit where you ought to be seated, dogs will occupy your seat.' So we need to be more cautious not to lose our seats because survival of the fittest is the universal law. I have stressed the importance of self-confidence several times, as essential to the process of making achievements.

34

Necessity is the mother of invention

> Any human being with average intelligence can generate new ideas.

My second son, Mithun once lost his balance and fell down while getting off the train after his journey from Thrissur. His twisted right leg eventually resulted in a sprained ankle. Due to severe pain and swelling, he was taken to hospital. Examining the X-ray, doctors spotted a slight rupture in the ligament. After casting the plaster, doctors recommended four weeks' complete bed rest for him.

All his plans to enjoy the summer holidays were upset by this small incident. Three days later, one fine morning, he asked me a very interesting question: "Daddy, why is there a difference in level between the railway platform and the train compartment? Is it a must? Why can't the platform be raised to the level of the compartment?"

The services of Indian Railways are availed of by lakhs and lakhs of people every day. But nobody might have raised this question or even thought of it. Only when Mithun was injured, he observed it closely and suggested a new idea. But others were not bothered about this outdated system of maintaining the railway platform and compartment doorsteps at different levels.

The human mind is capable of generating new ideas. We need not be reincarnated as Edison or Einstein for it. Any human being with average intelligence can generate new ideas. What is essential is the necessity and pressure. Otherwise, we are not likely to take it seriously. If we feel that our future is likely to be affected, we will definitely think about it and try to find out a solution. If we remain on the boundary wall of safety and comfort, we will never think of new avenues and opportunities. It has been observed that the maximum number of inventions had been made during the Second World War. Many of them were connected with defence requirements. But later, they became useful to the entire humanity.

If all the staff members of an organisation are really concerned about their organisation or are aware that their future prospects will depend on their performance, a number of suggestions will come from every one of them to improve the efficiency of its functioning. Unless we feel the pinch, we will not be alert. This is the common attitude of human beings and we can't blame anybody for it. In my opinion, we can get a lot of suggcstions on expenditure reduction, new ideas for marketing, reduction in travelling expenditure, telephone bills, operation with the availability of minimum stock, conservative use of stationery and raw materials, etc. To achieve this goal, officers and managers must create a healthy atmosphere and invite new ideas from other staff members. The proverb, 'Necessity is the mother of invention' has its own meaning and significance. There is no doubt about it.

35

A short pen is better than a long memory

Most of the people who are associated with our organisation, one way or another readily agree that V-Guard Industries is functioning very systematically and smoothly, like a well-oiled machine. The main ingredient of this achievement is proper planning. Without proper planning, nothing will be a success.

> Proper planning and systematic functioning are complementary to each other.

I have never come across a successful person who is not systematic and who acts without proper planning. If you know somebody like that, I would say that it is a great miracle. I do not believe in miracles. Proper planning and systematic functioning are complementary to each other. If a person is systematic, he will definitely be in the habit of planning future steps properly. Similarly, if a person has the habit of properly planning future steps, he is bound to be systematic. I am stressing more and more on this point because planning plays an important role in our life.

After all, a short pen is better than a long memory.

Proper planning is a must for a person to succeed. The examples that strike me first are those of a scribbling pad and pen and of course a diary. Some people have the mistaken notion that they have a good memory and they can memorise many things. But the fact is that a short pen is better than a long memory. It is better to scribble points frequently since ideas and suggestions strike your mind frequently irrespective of time and location. You may think that you can memorise the points for hours or days. It is not always true. If you have a scribbling pad and pen, why should you overload your brain? A diary may not always be available to you. But a scribbling pad and a pen can be kept with you to meet the demands of any situation. When you get a point, scribble it then and there. Don't hesitate to do it in front of strangers. Some people feel shy to do this under the impression that others may think they have a bad memory. So let me repeat the point that a short pen is better than a long memory.

When you get any instruction from your superiors, scribble it immediately. If you get some good suggestions from your juniors, note them down at once in front of them. This will give your juniors a feeling of importance. Make it a habit to transfer the points from the scribbling pad to the diary on a daily basis. Then your ideas, instructions from your superiors and suggestions from your juniors will be safe forever.

These days, many people use modern gadgets like i-pads and Notebooks to record their thoughts, even while travelling. Such innovations are to be used to our advantage to lead an organized life.

36

Lead a happy family life

In a letter published in the V-Guard House Magazine, "V & We", one of our business associates once sought my views on how to lead a happy family life. Very recently, one of my colleagues asked me to share my experience in grooming children. Analysing these important issues which complement each other, I feel that if children grow up to become successful individuals useful to the family and society, it is ample proof that their parents were leading a happy and systematic family life. Comparison can be drawn to any commercial product. By assessing the quality of a product, the public will get an idea of the industrial unit that manufactured it. In all probability, if the product is found to maintain high quality, the unit will be judged as a systematic, well-managed and quality-conscious organisation.

Happy and united families can bring up successful personalities and vice versa.

Naturally, happy and united families can bring up successful personalities and vice versa. In the character formation of an individual, the first 15 years of his life are very important. Parents are the role models for children. Knowingly or unknowingly, they imbibe many qualities of their father and mother. If you are a chain smoker and if you expect your children not to smoke, it is sheer foolishness.

If you want to hide any chinks in your character from your son, it is better to send him to a boarding school. If you want your children to imbibe many of your qualities, then let them grow up with you at least till they attain 15 years of age. I strongly oppose sending children to boarding schools to learn manners, etiquette and a good English accent. Under the pretext of giving better education in boarding schools, parents conveniently shirk their primary responsibility of grooming their children, and find more time to spend in social clubs or indulge in similar activities.

Until my children grow up to become successful citizens useful to society and the country, I cannot claim that I was leading a meaningful family life. I need to wait for some more years to judge myself. In this context, I have to congratulate my parents aged 82 and 76 who showed the way by leading a happy and successful family life. The result is that all their six children are very successful personalities, serving the society. I have thrown light on the magnificent qualities in their character which I am trying to imbibe, and pass on to the next generation. *(This was written in 1998).*

37

Discipline and etiquette

> Doing things at a reckless, 'Hurried' pace, will not take you to the goal easily.

During my visits to various countries, one important thing which I have noticed, is that the children there, are trained to be well-mannered, self-disciplined and taught to observe the rules of etiquette, right from primary school. They know that character formation begins from childhood, and children learn many things by watching their elders.

When we visit a crowded place like an amusement park in a developed country, we see a noticeable difference in the behaviour of people. All the visitors there are very self-disciplined. Here in Veega Land (Now re-named Wonderla, Kochi) we employ a large number of security staff to maintain law and order, and to ensure that the crowds move in orderly queues, at each ride. We hardly see a security person abroad! The ride operator comes out from the operator's cabin after a ride, directs the people in the queue to the ride, and goes back into the cabin to operate it. While he is inside the cabin, operating the ride, there is no one near the queue to ensure discipline. All of them wait patiently in a self-disciplined manner.

In Veega Land (Now re-named Wonderla, Kochi) and in other amusement parks in India, I have noticed that many people violate the queue system, resulting in quarrels, even though we provide security personnel to supervise. These types of unruly behaviour sometimes lead to manhandling, and the ride has to be stopped for a while until the issue is settled. Here, a small group of people creates inconvenience to the others, paralysing the entire operation. We must understand that in a crowded place, we should be self-disciplined and should obey the rules rather than making it necessary to enforce proper behaviour, so that everybody gets a fair chance, without interruption.

It is foolishness to run inside the bus to reach the destination fast.

Some people who are not self-disciplined always try to use short cut methods to achieve their goals, ignoring the inconvenience they cause to others. Doing things at a reckless, 'Hurried' pace, will not take you to the goal easily. Suppose we are travelling in a bus to a destination. For many reasons, sometimes the bus may run at a very slow speed. If anyone thinks, 'I will run inside the bus to reach my destination faster', it is sheer foolishness.

I think these simple lessons should be taught to children at home and schools. You can be selfish, but take a pledge 'I will not cause any inconvenience to others in any form or manner.' If everybody strictly follows this simple rule, our world would truly be Heaven on Earth. There will not be any wars between countries, no communal fights, no sound pollution, no water pollution, no air pollution, no cheating, no theft, no favouritism, no bribes, no dowry; the list is endless. In fact, no evils of any kind can flourish in such an environment!

38

Entrepreneurial tranquillity

If the captain of a cricket or football team feels that the match was won solely because of his merit, it is mere foolishness.

Once during an interview in 2002, a journalist asked me my age, he was astonished when I replied that I was almost 52. He said, "Normally, businessmen tend to look a lot older because of their tension and worry. But you look very young and pleasant, despite your age. What is the secret?" I replied, "First of all, let me admit that I am not a high profile businessman. When compared with leading businessmen like the Tatas, Birlas, Ambanis or many others, I am only a very small player in the industrial field. If I were in Bombay or Delhi, running a company with a turnover of 120 crores, no one would notice me there. Since Kerala is an industrially backward State and I happen to be stationed at Cochin, I get noticed here. In fact, I believe that it is not my merit, but Kerala's state as industrially backward, that has helped to project me as a successful businessman. It is a blessing in disguise. In Malayalam there is a saying, 'കുരുടൻ നാട്ടിൽ കോങ്കണ്ണൻ രാജാവ്,' which means, 'the squint-eyed person is King in the land of blind.'

But the press reporter persisted, "You still look much younger than many others in the same age group; what is the secret of your youthful appearance?" I then shared some of my views. I am usually a very relaxed person. I enjoy the work I do. I never think that I am doing any Herculean task, which no one else can undertake. I have committed many mistakes and some of them have been Himalayan blunders. But these have gone unnoticed in the backdrop of our

Group's overall success. I know that I am only an average person. In fact, I was only a mediocre student at school and college. It has taken me 25 long years to bring our group's turnover from 0 to 120 crores. Given the same facilities, some businessmen, might have expanded the business to a 1,200 crore company within the same time span. But I value peace of mind and happiness more than anything else. We all know the proverbial story of the hare and the tortoise. I consider myself a slow-moving person.

I believe that the achievements of the V-Guard Group are not entirely due to my abilities. If the captain of a cricket or football team feels that the match was won solely because of his merit, it is mere foolishness. Everybody knows that it is the result of a joint effort. I realise that our managers, officers, staff and other associates have played a major role in bringing the V-Guard group to this level. My role is only that of a team captain. In Malayalam there is a saying, '*ഉത്തരം താങ്ങുന്ന പല്ലിയെപ്പോലെ*' which means, 'The lizard which sits on the bottom of the beam, claims that it is holding up the entire roof.' If someone feels that he is great and responsible for everything, others will laugh at him.

39

Standing out in a world of look-alikes

> Only an original work will stand out in a world of look-alikes, and that is precisely what I had in my mind.

At last the countdown has begun! The long awaited date for the inauguration of Veega Land has been fixed – 3rd April, 2000. I have been waiting for an end to my long journey down this path that had begun some years before.

I conceived the idea of setting up a world-class amusement park in Kerala in 1997. Since then much water has flowed under the bridge. Many kids who were born during this period, must have started attending nursery school! In fact, I wanted to create a monument of my own, that would be useful to society and which would last for a long period, even after my time. I would like to be remembered by the coming generations in this manner, '*There once lived a man who always thought differently.*'

To become an outstanding member of society, one must have a combination of ambition, determination and a willingness to work hard. You cannot imagine the amount of time and energy, I have spent on this project right from the very beginning. When my wife noticed the growing pile of scribbled and crushed paper beside my table at home, she kept a bigger wastepaper basket nearby. In the initial stages, many people had some apprehensions about my ideas. They often asked questions like, "Will these Utopian ideas be materialized? Are you competent to do this independently? Are you going in for some kind of collaboration?"

An Original will always stand out among Copycats

I took up this major project mainly to satisfy my passion for civil and mechanical construction. It was also an ideal opportunity to implement my unique ideas on amusement and fun, even though I am not a qualified architect. As an investor, I could have engaged an internationally recognized firm, which is in the business of providing consultancy services and setting up amusement parks worldwide, as turnkey projects. That would have been safer and risk free with no bother to the investor. But the problem is that it would have been merely a copy of some park somewhere. It is always easy to create replicas, *however only an original work will stand out in a world of look-alikes, and that is precisely what I had in my mind.*

In order to implement my own ideas, the first thing I did, was to select a talented architect with no prior experience in designing amusement parks. Initially, we sat together for many hours, twice a week on a regular basis. We also had lengthy telephonic conversations in between, in order to give a final shape to my unique ideas. I have to congratulate him on the fact that he far exceeded my expectations in translating my dreams into reality.

Even after the construction work had begun, the original plan had to undergo many changes, taking into account the suggestions of our managers and supervisors. In the interim period, the project cost was revised thrice, and what you see there now, is the end result of a confluence of ideas from different minds.

40

Liberalisation

> Competition will compel industries to focus on research to produce quality items at a lower cost.

In June, 2000, at a grand function organised by the Income Tax Department, Union Minister of State for Finance, Sri Dhananjaya Kumar, presented awards to the top six taxpayers in the State. I am happy to note that, during the last six years, the Income Tax department has been giving due recognition to honest taxpayers in the country. Generally, all the government departments in our country have a suspicious and hostile attitude towards tax payers. They generally treat us all as if we are all tax evaders or criminals. There is a gradual change in their attitude. The government has started realising the importance of private enterprises.

Soon after independence, India developed a strong leaning towards socialism. We were more attached to the USSR than to the USA. Pandit Jawaharlal Nehru and many other Congress leaders of that time, thought that a variation of socialism* would be ideal for a country like India, where poverty is acute and the population is large. So the Income Tax rates were kept very high, around 80 to 90 percent. As a consequence, many people evaded tax payment and a parallel economy started flourishing. Similarly, corruption and underhand dealings also became rampant.

To add fuel to the fire, there were restrictions on production of all items like four-wheelers, two-wheelers, etc. As a result, misappropriation became a regular practice in every field. For example, licences were given only to two companies to manufacture scooters.

There were also quantitative restrictions on annual productions. Since there was no competition, there was no motivation to produce better items. Customers had to stand in queues to book a scooter or any other vehicle.

Now because of liberalisation, things have changed a lot. If the resources and the necessary technology are available, anyone can produce any item. The Indian market is now flooded with a number of high quality brands. Today, customers have a better choice of goods and services, that too at a lower price because of the prevailing competition. It is now the turn of marketing executives to stand in queues at the customer's doorstep to secure orders for their products.

As far as economic policy and commercial ventures are concerned, I feel that India is moving in the right direction. Competition will compel industries to focus on research to produce quality items at a lower cost. In the changed set up, customers are benefitted more. They get real value for their money.

* The avedi session of the Indian National Congress adopted, "Socialistic pattern of Society" as the party policy

41

The bane of productivity

> No industrialist will be interested in running a unit by giving up his self esteem even if the unit is making a profit.

Everybody agrees that as long as Keralites are working outside Kerala, they are very hard-working, disciplined and very productive. But once they are in Kerala, it is just the opposite.

This is the only state in India with 100 per cent literacy. The living conditions of unskilled workers here are far, far better than those in any other state. But because of fewer job opportunities, we have the highest percentage of unemployed educated youth. The wage levels here are very high. Those who are already employed are enjoying the maximum benefits by means of bargaining with the support of trade union leaders. A combination of high wages, low productivity and the undisciplined attitude of workers have made Kerala the least attractive location for industrialists to start new ventures.

In the process of bargaining for higher wages, trade union leaders have indirectly encouraged indiscipline and low productivity. To attract large groups of workers to their unions, the leaders draw a glossy picture about the rights of workers, but in that process, they purposely avoid drawing their attention to their duties. Unless there is discipline and productivity among workers, who would be interested in running an industrial unit?

A qualified person who aspires to start a unit by selling his family property to raise money for investment and to create some job opportunities will be dubbed as a bloodsucker, out to exploit workers.

For their own existence and survival, union leaders deliberately create a gap between the workers and the owners of an industrial unit.

In the early stages of a small-scale venture, when there is no union, the 'hero' of the workers will be their own proprietor. Workers will talk highly about their organisation and its proprietor. But once there is interference by union leaders from outside, their attitude will turn upside down. After that, the proprietor will be seen as the greatest enemy of the workers! I am writing this from my own experience.

Union leaders and workers often forget the basic truth that no industrialist will be interested in running a unit by giving up his self esteem even if the unit is making a profit. Unless there is a conducive atmosphere, he will look for alternative avenues for his existence.

Ultimately, union leaders and workers will realise the fact that they are cutting the very branch of the tree on which they are seated. But very often, this realisation comes too late.

42

Money order economy

In a way, the labour unrest we faced earlier proved to be a blessing in disguise since it paved the way for launching our present system of production, involving the association of various outside units. Instead of concentrating on marketing and ensuring better quality of their products, industrialists in Kerala are wasting their valuable time by arguing with trade union leaders.

> Industrialists in Kerala are wasting their valuable time by arguing with trade union leaders.

The Government of Kerala claims that militant trade unionism is now a thing of the past. According to the Government, there is here now a conducive atmosphere for industries to flourish. If this is true, why aren't people investing in Kerala? For example, one of the biggest tyre manufacturing firms in India, is owned by Keralites. It banks on Kerala for raw materials. Yet, why is it that the company has no interest in starting new units in Kerala? How much effort has our government made to pressurise the managements of many companies to reopen their closed factories? Why are they not interested in reopening them?

Kerala now enjoys a 'money order economy' thanks to the contributions made by lakhs and lakhs of Keralites working abroad and in some North Indian cities. No trade union leader in Kerala can offer job security to those NRIs and Keralites working in other states. 'Hire and fire' is the labour policy in all the developed capitalist economies of the world. Socialism has been a failure all over the world. Survival of the fittest is the order of the day. In India because of liberalisation, many industries are facing stiff competition from cheaper products coming from different parts of the world.

Unskilled migrant workers from Tamil Nadu look upon Kerala as their 'Gulf'. Can we prevent their flow into the state? Due to the high rate of literacy, Keralites seek only white collar jobs. Can any union leader prevent an industrialist from closing his factory in Kerala and moving to another state? Can we put up fencing on our State boundaries to prevent this?

My most recent experience of labour troubles was at the construction site of our amusement park. Within just one year, there were three episodes of labour unrest at the site as a result of which a total of 45 working days were lost. These disputes were not about increasing daily wages. On two occasions the trade unions fought over the issue of determining the percentage of employees from each union. The third fight was over a disciplinary issue. Two headload workers had misbehaved with the supervisors and the management had terminated their services.

In each case, we were forced to approach the Hon'ble High Court for getting police protection to resume work. As usual, the authorities were watching the 'tamasha' (fun) just as a mother cat watches her kitten playing with a half-dead rat. Fortunately the work at our amusement park was completed in time without too many problems.

43

Hardcore self-motivation

> For motivation to be effective, it must be sincere and heartfelt.

Twenty five years after the inception of V-Guard, when I look back, it gives me immense satisfaction to realise that I could fulfil many ambitions in life. On this happy occasion of our Silver Jubilee year (2002), I have to thank all the staff members, managers, manufacturing units, raw material suppliers, distributors, dealers, financial institutions, consultants, government officials, politicians, the media, friends, relatives and all other well-wishers who gave me their unstinting support to bring the V-Guard group to these heights. All the print and electronic media in Kerala, have given a very good and extensive coverage of our achievements. They wrote and spoke very highly of me and the organisation, and this has motivated me to do something more for society. Motivating words are the fuel which will impel any individual to achieve higher goals.

When we talk about motivation, we know that everyone is trying to excel in his own life and to become a successful person in any walk of life. Anyone who earnestly seeks to be successful must know the art of motivating himself, and motivating others. Unless you yourself are motivated, you cannot motivate others. All of us know that a bright future is reserved for progressive thinkers, dreamers, and doers. If you think you can, you can. If you think you cannot, you cannot. If we analyse any success story, we learn that, invariably it is the person's attitude towards crisis situations that determines his success. He will always find alternative methods to solve problems. Creating a positive, stimulating and motivating environment is very important for success. Most people would like to have it, but don't know how to go about acquiring these skills. If these were readily available for sale in the market, in a ready-to-use form, there will certainly be many buyers.

On average, I would say that only about 5% of the general population has developed to the extent required, to be called a real success. These are the self motivating high achievers who know the art of motivating their subordinates. Many people know this truth, but fail to translate their ideas into practice. Let me ask you a question; have you ever met a successful person who has come up in life through sheer luck, and who is not included in the above category? Without doubt, the answer is a resounding 'No'. Ensuring long-term success is like running a marathon, not a 100 metres dash or sprint.

Her desire that her child has to come up in life is so strong.

You may be eager to know how I learned these skills. The answer is, by closely observing successful people and their attitude towards problems, by attending personality development training programmes and by reading management books. From all these, I learned that the key factor is motivating your subordinates. Look at a mother and her one-year-old child who is about to walk. Her desire to see her child come up in life is very strong and it comes out of unconditional love. We need that type of commitment. For motivation to be effective, it must be sincere and heartfelt. Then you can see the difference! (*Written in 2002*)

44

Brand name

> While selecting a brand name, it is better to avoid tongue twisters and names with too many alphabets.

A small scale industrialist once asked me to explain why we selected the name 'V-Guard' and wanted to know what should be the main considerations in choosing a brand name.

As you all know, V-Guard was launched with a single product, namely stabilizers. I was looking for a simple name to represent the product's function i.e. 'Guarding against voltage fluctuation'. The letter 'V' is widely used for voltage in physics and electrical engineering. It was thus that the name 'V-Guard' emerged. With the passage of time, the public started associating the letter 'V' with 'Victory' or 'We'. Naturally, when we introduced new products, the brand name was easily accepted by the public.

Frankly speaking, the original meaning of 'V-Guard' has nothing to do with our new products like clocks, pumps, water heaters and so on. But this does not really matter, because once a brand name is established, the public is not bothered about its real meaning. For example, all of you are familiar with the name D.C.M. Toyota, well known in the automobile industry. But not many of you know that the letters D.C.M. stand for 'Delhi Cloth Mills'. Earlier, DCM was manufacturing

cloth. But the name had nothing to do with their truck division formed in collaboration with Toyota of Japan.

Similarly, the name we chose for our amusement park 'VEEGA' has no real meaning. It is only a set of alphabets bearing some resemblance with 'V-Guard' in pronunciation. My humble suggestion is that while selecting a brand name, it is better to avoid tongue twisters and names with too many alphabets.

When I selected the name 'V-Guard', I never imagined that this brand name would eventually secure a national image. But when I look back now, I can see some positive factors in selecting the name which helped the brand to remain unique.

Now, many companies have a tendency to copy or imitate the names of leading brands in the market. When we started manufacturing stabilizers, the leading brands were Keltron, Nelco, Transtab, Telics, etc. I am proud to say that I never attempted to copy or imitate any of them. This, I am happy to say, is one of the major reasons for the success of V-Guard. Many years have gone by since we launched our first product. Since then, many brands of stabilizers have hit the market with brand names resembling ours and beginning with the letter 'V'.

If a new entrant into the market plans to copy or imitate the existing brand names, it is a clear signal to the public that these are merely 'copy cats' who excel in copying names, designs and even the technology used by brand leaders.

Obviously, such products will have nothing unique or distinctive about them. So, it is always better to establish one's own identity in the market, which may be difficult in the initial stages but will certainly pay rich dividends later.

45

Branding – a careful approach

> We have no way of physically verifying the quality and quantity of a given item. There lies the importance of brand names.

I have already written about considering certain factors while building a brand name. Nowadays, it is very essential to have a brand image to sell a product in large quantities. When we go to a supermarket, we generally prefer to select items by their brand name, rather than physically checking their quality. Since most of them are already packed, we simply select them, take them from the rack and put them in the basket. We have no way of physically verifying the quality and quantity of a given item. There lies the importance of brand names. When we step into a shop, we have some preconceived notions about the quality and reliability of certain brands, and this is reflected in our buying patterns. Here, I am trying to convince you about the importance of a brand name when selling an item.

Suppose your wife has conceived and you are expecting a baby in the near future. With a lot of enthusiasm and excitement, you and your wife start searching for the most beautiful name for your child. Similarly, an entrepreneur who conceives a new idea to start a business, goes through the same kind of experience. Every brand owner wishes to select the best and most attractive name for his product. Over the last 25 years my experience of closely observing the rise and fall of a number of brand names in the market, has helped me to form some ideas or take tips for creating a new brand name.

In selecting a new brand name, we must take care to ensure that the selected word is the simplest one possible, to read and write. I know the difficulty that North Indians and foreigners experience in pronouncing my name, 'Kochouseph'. Let your product name be such that even small children can pronounce it easily. This will definitely help you to spread the popularity of the brand quickly. It would be better if you can find a proper noun, which is not found in any dictionary, rather than deciding on common nouns like 'Premier', 'Popular', etc. If you take a word like 'Premier', you can find an umpteen number of products in the market which bear this name, including tyres, chappals, cars and so on. In such cases, the identity is not clear. Again, if you have selected a common noun, someone else might have already used it as a brand name somewhere, in some other part of the country. Later on, you may find it difficult to get the brand name registered for exclusive ownership.

Some people choose their family name as a brand name. Here, you have to remember that all other members in your family have the right to use the same name, and you cannot prevent them legally from doing so. Today, many members belonging to prominent business families are using their family name, and latecomers are taking advantage of the reputation built up by earlier entrants. Over a period of many years, you are going to invest crores and crores of rupees on the name you have selected for brand building. So, be careful while choosing a brand name. Shakespeare asked, "After all, what's in a name?" But in the matter of deciding on brand names, one has to consider many things!!

46

Brand building

> Remember, we cannot fool the public for a long period by advertisements alone.

I was once invited to speak at a seminar, to share my experiences of building a brand name. After receiving the invitation, I began to think about the subject analytically, 'What are the major factors that can be attributed to building a good brand image?' After spending many weeks reflecting on the subject, I gathered some ideas on the topic.

We can compare a brand name with a hot air balloon, which needs continuous heating of air to inflate, and sustain it at high altitudes. Similarly, to boost the image of a brand name and sustain it in the market, advertisement & sales promotion activities must be carried out on a continuous basis. The navigator of the balloon must be very conscious and alert when adjusting the throttle of the burner and guiding the balloon in the desired direction. Otherwise, it may hit a mountain or a high tension electric tower. Similarly, the top management of an organisation must be very vigilant, and has to identify and formulate the correct strategy for product innovation, quality assurance and customer care. The choice of suitable words and appropriate media for advertisement, has an impact on the effectiveness of an advertisement campaign.

It can be very dangerous if a hole develops in the balloon, and depending on the size of the hole, it will descend steeply even if the throttle of the burner is fully opened. Similarly, if there is a problem in the quality of the product, or in after-sale service, the negative publicity spreads rapidly like wildfire and affects the reputation of

We can compare a brand name to a hot air balloon.

the brand, even if you advertise heavily in all the media. Remember, we cannot fool the public for a long period by advertisements alone. If the product is inferior, it will be a futile bid to promote the brand image by hiring even a well-known personality like Aiswarya Rai as a brand ambassador.

Again, when we talk about brand image, we often see that some companies are eager to discredit their competitors through their advertisements. They always try to project the defects of their competitors, and in the process, forget to highlight their own special merits. As we know, people generally tend to dislike those who criticize others. The same rule applies to brand names also; the public tends to develop an aversion to those companies which always criticize their competitors.

Recently, I came across the advertisement of an audio system which claimed, in bold letters, that if you bought the product, you would get 2 free tickets to a Ganamela (music concert) by Yesudas. When I read the remaining part of the advertisement, the fine print revealed that the free gift was in fact, only two audio cassettes of Yesudas's songs! I felt cheated, and had wasted my time reading the whole advertisement. Making tall claims, by which I mean making grossly exaggerated statements about the company or its products, will always have a negative impact. People will easily identify boastful statements and will develop an aversion to those brands that make such claims.

47

Poor self-esteem

> The mission of an entrepreneur is to win and retain the leadership position in the market, and not to fight with other companies in the same field.

I would like to examine some more aspects relating to the importance of brand names. In this context, I wish to narrate an incident which relates to this topic. A few years back, I happened to meet a small-scale pump manufacturer, based in Coimbatore, who was proud to say that his pump sets carried the brand name, 'Allwyn'. I was surprised to hear this, because everyone knew that 'Allwyn' was a registered trade mark of a company in Hyderabad, which made refrigerators and watches. How then, could someone else use the same name? He declared triumphantly that he had fought a long-drawn legal battle with 'Allwyn', and had finally won the case in court because 'Allwyn' in Hyderabad, had registered their brand only for refrigerators and watches. So he found a loophole and finally won the case. He was very enthusiastic about narrating how he fought the case for a long time.

But my thoughts on the subject were different. Why should he try to take the credit for someone else's goodwill, which had been painstakingly created by the brand owner over a period of time? Why couldn't he build a new, unique brand name of his own, and establish a separate identity? Why should he copy others? The public will easily rate his company's products as imitations. Companies which follow such practices can never flourish in the field and become market leaders. I believe that the mission of an entrepreneur is to win and retain the leadership position in the market, and not to fight with other companies in the same field.

One can see shops in Delhi's Chandini Chowk area, selling duplicate fans, voltage stabilizers, etc. under popular brand names. In many cases these sellers of duplicate items never face any kind of resistance from the brand owners. Please remember that we could crack down, with the help of the Bangalore police, on a bogus company which was manufacturing a product called 'petrol saver' under the brand name 'V-Guard', whose logo was an exact replica of our own. A detailed study revealed that the product had none of the qualities claimed by the company; it was a clear instance of cheating. Similarly, we were recently able to stop another company manufacturing chappals under the name 'V-Star', in Kerala.

Suppressing one's identity by wearing a mask and projecting another's goodwill, will not last long.

I recall another instance when the manager of a travel agency came to my residence. My wife Shiela had given him a warm welcome, since she was under the impression that he came from a reputed international airline called KLM, which is a leading Dutch airline company with an established reputation. After a brief conversation, it was revealed that the company which he represented, was only a Cochin based travel agency which was run by an individual. The manager had come to my residence to canvass business. In my opinion, such practices are akin to wearing a mask; suppressing one's true identity and capitalizing on goodwill that rightfully belongs to others. But such tactics will not yield results for long.

48

A satisfied customer is the best advertising medium

A satisfied customer will be an indirect propagandist of a product.

Many people are under the impression that the name V-Guard, today is a household name only because of our advertising strategy and sales promotion campaigns. Yes, of course, we regularly advertise through all the media and spend a good deal of money in the process. For example, in 1997 alone, we spent around Rs. 3.5 crore for the purpose which was just under 5 per cent of the year's turnover of Rs. 75 crore.

I certainly agree that advertisements are essential to propagate the merits of a product to a large group of people. However, I strongly believe that the reputation V-Guard enjoys now is not just due to the advertisements. In fact, the major contributing factors are continuous efforts in maintaining the quality of the products, and a sustained commitment to giving proper after-sale service.

A satisfied customer will be an indirect propagandist of a product. If he is happy with the quality of the product and after-sale service, it is basic human nature that he will use every opportunity to recommend the product to others. Conversely, an unhappy customer will do just the opposite. Before going to buy a costly product, we all tend to gather the opinions of our friends, relatives and colleagues about different brands of an item instead of blindly depending on advertisements. If they have had any bitter experience with a particular brand, either in quality or after-sale service, they will dissuade you from buying it. To understand this simple theory, the brand name owner need not be a management wizard. 'Bad news spread easily like wild fire' and 'we cannot cheat people for a long period' are simple universal truths.

If an industrialist believes that he can sell inferior quality products through heavy advertisements, which will sustain him in the market for long, then he is a fool. Starting a tiny small scale unit, establishing a brand name and nurturing it into a medium scale one, is like planting and nursing a coconut sapling. It will take its own sweet time and much water has to flow under the bridge before it can yield any fruit. The advantage is that if you maintain it properly, you will get the yield for a longer period. It is easy to plant a plantain sapling which will yield fruit within one year, but the yield will be available only for a short term.

49

Hostage at home

> I have to thank viral fever because I have got many more classic ideas.

During the first week of March, 2002, I was virtually under 'house arrest' for seven days when I was down with Viral Fever. I rarely fall ill, but this time I was compelled to undergo a long-term 'imprisonment' due to the fever. However, I never felt any monotony or sense of isolation on those days. My favourite T.V channels, National Geographic, Discovery Channel, Animal Planet and A.X.N were a great source of relief during this period. Personally, I do not enjoy watching Malayalam serials on television, even though we regularly advertise our products in those prime time slots. I believe that we neither get any meaningful message, nor derive knowledge or pleasure by watching those episodes. But if you watch the channels I mentioned earlier, you will certainly feel that you are in a different world.

'I was under house arrest for 7 days.'

For example, on the 'Discovery' and 'National Geographic' channels there are programmes like 'Travel Time', which is essentially an armchair travelogue that takes you to different locations in the world, which are rich in tourist attractions. You can see and enjoy the sights and sounds of various locales and listen to excellent narrations which describe different parts of the world, without spending money on air tickets or other travel expenditure. When we watch 'Animal Planet' and other wildlife programmes on 'Discovery' and 'National Geographic' we will be amazed to see the behavioural pattern of different animals, birds and other underwater creatures. Their food patterns, survival techniques and habits are really fascinating to watch.

The painstaking efforts and patience of the cameramen and crew, in taking each shot should be appreciated. We will be astonished at the courage shown by these cameramen, to video-tape some breathtaking sequences under extremely dangerous situations. I believe that if we regularly watch such channels, our knowledge about animals, birds, underwater creatures and bio-diversities will increase ten-fold.

On the 'Discovery Channel', there is a programme called 'Extreme Machines' and a similar one on 'The National Geographic' called 'Human Edge', which present the latest inventions in the world. Sometimes, they show advanced Amusement Rides like the high speed hanging Roller Coasters, Vertical fall from a tower as high as a 60-storeyed building and many other amazing feats. On the AXN Channel some special programmes like 'Who Dares Wins', 'Ripley's Believe It or Not', 'Amazing Videos', etc will take you into a different world. You have to watch these programmes and enjoy the experience, since their uniqueness cannot be explained by mere words alone. Similarly, other programmes like 'Crime Files', 'FBI Files' and 'Medical Detectives' will introduce you to the latest techniques which are used to unravel the mysteries of crime and to nab the culprits, without using any third-rate methods of extracting confessions by physical torture.

I have explained so much about these channels to generate some interest in you, so that you feel the urge to watch them. Television serials are pure fiction, and based on the imagination of the scriptwriter, whereas here, you see real-life stories and actual situations. If you can generate interest among children to watch these channels, their general knowledge will increase considerably. Personally speaking, I have benefited greatly by watching them. I was able to get many ideas for landscaping and elevation of buildings and rides, which I have implemented in Veega Land. So, in a sense, I have to thank Viral Fever because I have got many more classic ideas, which can be incorporated in the future expansion of our park.

50

Do your duties first

> To find a solution to a problem, you must have peace of mind and self-confidence to analyze it and overcome the difficulty.

Many of you would have observed that nowadays, online lotteries are becoming increasingly popular. In fact, the long queues of youngsters at the ticket counters is a clear indication of this. As you know, many people are eager to indulge in get-rich-quick schemes, which generally tend to attract lazy people who are tempted to try their luck. This reminds me of a story about a lazy man, who always prayed to God to let him win a lottery bumper prize. Although he was lazy and irresponsible, he would visit the church daily and pray, "Oh God, I have been a good man, and haven't inconvenienced anyone. I have also served you well. And yet, till now, I could neither acquire wealth, nor ensure a regular monthly income for myself. I need a little help; let me win a lottery. I have only a small request; one lucky number, that is all." And so, day after day, week after week, he continued his prayers, but nothing happened.

Finally, he became frustrated and desperate. Raising his voice, he looked up and prayed, "Please God, I have been praying and waiting for weeks; please have mercy on me." Suddenly, the clouds parted and the booming voice of God echoed down from the sky, "This time I am ready but you are not. You are so lazy and irresponsible that you never even bothered to purchase a ticket!" The moral of the story is this; if you want to win the lottery, the first thing you need to do, is to buy a ticket at least. If you are lazy and irresponsible, even Almighty God

"You are so lazy and irresponsible that you never even bothered to purchase a ticket!"

cannot save you. In Malayalam, there is a saying, which goes thus: '*താൻ പാതി, ദൈവം പാതി*', which means 'First, you will have to finish the task on your own, only then will God help you to get the result.' Unless you do your duties properly, which God, in which religion, can grant your wishes or bestow great fortune upon you?

I know many people who have never believed in God, but have been successful in life. They work hard and do their duties promptly. They have enough self-confidence to handle any setbacks, and maintain a positive attitude towards the future. With such a mindset, it is only natural that they will be successful. On the other hand, there are those who always curse themselves and keep saying, "I am an unlucky person, this is my fate; you people are the lucky ones. Why is God giving me all these difficulties?" and so on. I believe that one day or another, there will be setbacks in everybody's life. It is the ability of a person to go through difficult life-situations, without feeling frustrated and dejected, which makes him successful in life. My attitude is that 'there is always light at the end of the tunnel.' There will be a solution to any problem. But to find the solution, you must have peace of mind and self-confidence to analyse the problem and overcome the difficulty.

51

There is strength in numbers

> Any successful organisation is the result of the joint efforts of a large group of people at various levels and in different departments.

While appraising the improvements carried out at Veega Land (Now re-named Wonderla, Kochi) I was quite surprised to note that more than 300 changes have been implemented at the park since its inauguration, during the first three years itself. This does not include the installation of new rides or slides. There have been numerous minor changes or corrections done on the pathways, steps, ramps, and also at the restaurants, toilets, changing rooms and other facilities. All these changes came about as a result of suggestions made by our customers, managers and staff members of Veega Land (Now re-named Wonderla, Kochi). They all really felt the need for such changes. Similarly, many improvements and corrections were put into effect, in our guest relations policy; in the variety of food served, and so on. Today, I am really proud that Veega Land (Now re-named Wonderla, Kochi) has become more customer friendly, and we get many letters of appreciation from our visitors. This reminds me of the words of the great philosopher John Ruskin, 'Quality is never an accident; there must be the will to produce a superior thing.' We are all familiar with the proverb, 'If there is a will, there is a way.' Now, if we combine these two statements, the idea conveyed would be that, if we have a strong desire, we can create a superior quality product or facility. It is indeed true that in any endeavour, everything depends on our 'will'.

During the early years of V-Guard, when I personally designed the cartons of our stabilizers, without the help of any professional advertising agencies, I had the words of John Ruskin printed on them in a prominent manner, because they had influenced me deeply. It goes without saying, that unless we are quality conscious, we cannot survive in the current climate of intense competition. Any successful organisation is the result of the joint efforts of a large group of people at various levels and in different departments. However intelligent and smart one may be, unless one is ready to work as a member of a

Dear son, put in all your efforts to remove the block.

team, there will be limits to one's productivity. When many minds work together in a team, the results will be unbelievable.

This reminds me of the story of a father and son who went for an evening walk. On the way, they saw a large stone lying in the middle of the road, blocking the way. The father said to his son, "Put in all your efforts and remove the stone, so that traffic will not be blocked." As suggested, the son went ahead and tried to remove the stone, but it was so big that the boy could not move it. His father stood aside and watched as he tried in vain to remove it. Finally, the boy came back and said to his father, "The stone is so big that I cannot move it." The father urged him on, "Put in all your efforts and try again." So the boy struggled hard, but came back exhausted and explained his helplessness. His father replied, "When I said 'put in all your efforts',

I did not mean that you should rely solely on your own physical effort; you could have also tried to mobilize other people's help, including mine, to move the stone. You could have asked me and the other pedestrians to lend a hand, so that jointly, the task would be easy."

The moral of the story is very simple. There are limits to the capability of an individual. But when he works in a group, the results will be astonishing.

52

Luck and ill-luck

Remain calm and maintain presence of mind, to find solutions to problems.

Once while addressing a large gathering of college students in elhi recently, our former Rashtrapathi Sri A. P. J. Abdul Kalam said, "The fear of failure is the main stumbling block to success and excellence." Individually, all of us wish to become successful persons in our fields. But, apprehensive attitudes such as, 'I am not capable'; 'I am not lucky'; 'I fear that I cannot complete the task'; 'I may fail', etc., are the main stumbling blocks that retard, or even prevent the growth of an individual. Our President, a successful scientist by profession, knows the importance of self-confidence and a positive thinking attitude, which determines an individual's success. When we analyze the basic mindset of successful people, it is clear that these elements are very predominant in their character.

This reminds me of an incident in the life of the great Napoleon Bonaparte. In a battle, Napoleon's army was once encircled by enemy troops and was about to surrender. There was not enough food and water in their camps. Even under such alarming circumstances, Napoleon was sleeping peacefully, unmoved by the prospect of the impending defeat. In the meanwhile, all the army captains and generals were clearly worried and ran around inside the camps, in total disarray. Finally, they were compelled to wake up Napoleon from his sleep, and said, "Sir, we are in deep trouble. There is no food and water in our camp. We are about to be defeated." Despite hearing these words, Napoleon maintained his composure. He yawned and said, "No, I don't

Sir, please wake up, we are in deep trouble.

agree; there is plenty of food and water nearby." While the generals and captains looked at each other, bewildered at his remarks, he added, "These are in abundant supply within the enemy camp. Let's capture the enemy so that we will achieve two goals in one go." History reveals that Napoleon won a resounding victory in that particular battle.

If we can stay calm and collected in crisis situations, 99.9% of the problems encountered can be solved in our favour. We need to remain calm and maintain presence of mind, in order to find alternative solutions to problems. It is imperative that alternative methods are tried out, in the problem-solving process. In many critical situations, we may lose our confidence, which, will severely affect our decision-making. In Malayalam there is a saying 'പേടിച്ചാൽ ഒളിക്കാൻ ഇടമില്ല', which means if you are frightened, you will feel unsafe even in the safest place. But if we are bold and daring, problem-solving becomes much easier. Right from our childhood, we have been hearing that, 'Failures are the stepping stones to success' and we know that it is quite true. But when we really experience a failure, we forget these inspiring words, get frustrated, and never make another attempt. That is precisely why our former Rashtrapathi said 'Fear of failure' is the main hurdle in the pursuit of success and excellence.

About the Author

Kochouseph Chittilappilly was born in 1950 in Thrissur District, Kerala into a family which was traditionally engaged in agriculture. He holds a Master's Degree in Physics and began his career as a Supervisor in an electronics company.

At the age of 27, he started a modest SSI Unit manufacturing and selling stabilizers with just 2 workers. Now V-Guard is a listed company with various electrical, electronic and electro-mechanical products with a turnover of more than 1000 crores.

In the year 2000, he started an amusement park in the name '*Veega Land*' (now known as Wonderla, Kochi), which has now become one of the most attractive destinations in Kerala. The success story of the said Park made him to venture another amusement park, '*Wonderla*', in Bangalore, which is the biggest amusement park in India.

Kochouseph Chittilappilly is the recipient of numerous awards, which were bestowed on him for his exemplary performance in business. Besides Practical Wisdom 1 and Practical Wisdom 2 which exemplify effective ways of practical management in business as well as in real life, he has authored *Ormakkilivathil* (Malayalam) – A true life memoir of his younger days.

He was also chosen as the Manorama – Newsmaker of the Year 2011.

Mr. Chittilappilly is also a humanitarian par excellence. He donated one of his kidney's to a poor and needy truck driver whom he had never met before. Along with a charitable institution based in Kerala, The Kidney Federation of India, Kochouseph formed a kidney chain-the first of its kind in India, wherein he started the chain with his donation and one close relative of the recipient will donate her kidney and the next recipient's relative would donate further, thereby carrying forward this unique kidney chain.

His hobbies include listening to music, reading and watching documentaries in informative channels. He is married to Sheela who is heading and managing '*V-Star Creations*' the apparel division of V-Guard group.

The couple is blessed with two sons – Arun and Mithun. Arun is the Managing Director of 'Wonder La' and his wife Priya is the Executive Director of 'Wonder La'. Mithun is the Managing Director of V-Guard Industries Ltd and his wife Joshna is the Executive Director of V-Star Creations.

Now the second generation is actively involved in the family business and Kochouseph likes to spend a good amount of his time in philanthropic activities.